WHAT ARE THEY SAYING ABOUT
MYSTICISM?

What Are They Saying About Mysticism?

Harvey D. Egan, S.J.

PAULIST PRESS
New York/Ramsey

Library of Congress
Catalog Card Number: 82-81195

ISBN: 0-8091-2459-9

Published by Paulist Press
545 Island Road, Ramsey, N.J. 07446

Printed and bound in the
United States of America

24251

Contents

Introduction

The topic "mysticism" frequently evokes strong reactions. Mass media tend to treat mysticism as allegedly dealing with the unreal, the abstract, the vague, the poetic, the emotional, the parapsychological, or even the "spooky." Many Christians have problems with mysticism. For those influenced by the Continental-European Protestant theologians, such as Ritschl, Troelsch, Nygren, von Harnack, Barth, Brunner, and Bultmann, mysticism means little more than Greek-infested, heretical Christianity. Some in the Catholic tradition regard mysticism as a dangerous path reserved for an elite who have ecstasies, visions, hear heavenly voices, receive the stigmata, levitate, and so on. They would counsel forgetting about mysticism and walking the safe path of the sacraments, devotion, dogma, and authority.

Defining the word mysticism is no easy task. At the turn of the century, one noted scholar of mysticism, William Ralph Inge,[1] listed twenty-six different definitions. To do full justice to the contemporary interest and research in the mystical traditions of the East and West, psychology, the occult, altered states of consciousness, psychedelic drug experiences, charismatic phenomena, etc., would perhaps require listing several hundred, often irreconcilable definitions of mysticism.

The old term "mystical" was associated with the Eleusinian, Orphic, and Dionysian mystery religions which flourished in the Greco-Roman world in the early years of Christianity. The mystic

1

(*mustes*) had to keep silent, to keep his mouth shut (*muein*), about the secret rites into which he was initiated. The word passed into the neo-Platonic tradition and referred to the deliberate closing of the eyes to all external things to complete divine Wisdom within. The term *muo* was used of the closed eyes of someone in ecstatic, neo-Platonic contemplation of eternal Truth seen only with the internal eyes.

The word *mystica* came into Christianity by way of the famous late fifth-century Syrian monk, Pseudo-Dionysius, who wrote the mystical classic, *Mystica Theologia*. For him, mysticism involved the secrecy of the mind or that trans-conceptual state of consciousness which experiences God as a ray of divine Darkness. Recent commentators have also noted the influence of the first-century Jewish neo-Platonist, Philo, upon Christian mysticism. He combined Jewish belief and Greek thought and emphasized God's secret counsels.

Although the word mysticism is not found in Scripture, the Greek New Testament word *mysterion* is used to signify what many today consider mysticism to involve: the hidden presence of God and Christ in Scripture, the sacraments, and the events of daily life. Many early Christian theologians, moreover, considered exegesis properly done to be mystical contemplation, or experiential tasting of the divine reality brought about by Christ. For the Fathers of the Church, as Louis Bouyer says, mysticism

> is always the experience of an invisible objective world: the world whose coming the Scriptures reveal to us in Jesus Christ, the world into which we enter, ontologically, through the liturgy, through the same Jesus Christ ever present in the Church.[2]

Contemporary use of the terms "mysticism," "mystic," and "mystical" usually focuses upon the human potential for direct and immediate experience of the Absolute, the teachings and systems of living developed by the mystics, and the whole gamut of persons, experiences, teachings, traditions, life styles, etc., involved with these. Although this book will present authors who define mysticism in a vast variety of ways, perhaps mysticism can be tentatively defined as the universal thrust of the human spirit for experiential union with the Absolute and the theory of that union.

Few contemporary commentators identify mysticism with the occult, witchcraft, or the parapsychological; only a few view it as regressive, pathological behavior involving escape from the world and repressed eroticism. Some, however, focus on mysticism almost exclusively as a psychological moment of inspired rapture. More and more writers, on the other hand, see religious mysticism as the intensification and full flowering of authentic religious living. An increasing number, too, emphasize that all genuine mysticism, be it Christian or non-Christian, religious or non-religious, is actually authentic human living.

The great religious mystics of the ages have been those giants of humanity haunted by, purified by, illuminated by, and finally united to and transformed into Truth and Love. Having renounced all, they claimed to have found all. They have made the astonishing assertion that they have the answer to life. They have lived their lives in such a way, moreover, as to make that claim credible. Having cut through the pain, misery, selfishness, and brokenness of life, they have "hit bottom" to discover the God of Truth and Love at the root of all things. They became experientially convinced that life has a deeply beautiful ultimate meaning in Truth and Love. Along with this, they are paradigms of human authenticity who love Truth, Love, and their brothers and sisters. Common sense, practicality, social and political action, compassion, dedicated service of humanity, and mercy also stamp the lives of these great lovers.

The mystics have much to say, therefore, about who and what we are. All of us are at least potential mystics; most of us, with their help, can discover mysticism in our own lives and in the lives of those with whom we live and work. The great mystics are the paradigms and the amplifiers of a life of deep faith, hope, and love. They help us to hear the interior whispers and to see the faint flickers of truth and love in ourselves and others. By looking at their lives, we can frequently discover the obstacle in us to fully authentic human life. Looking into the lives of the great mystics will help to locate the compass of our hearts, to see what authentic human living is, and what our final purification, illumination, and transformation

entail. The mystics are living books on authentic human living and
eschatology.

The purpose of this book, therefore, is to present the manifold
approaches to mysticism taken by recent and contemporary commentators. It will present the main lines of contemporary mystical
scholarship by offering as many positions and counterpositions on
mysticism as the scope of this series allows.

The first two chapters will center upon those who examine the
psychological dimension of mysticism. Their views range from explaining mysticism as a pathological, regressive phenomenon to one
involving the highest levels of human consciousness, open to and
requiring religious interpretation.

Chapter 3 denies the contemporary thesis that all mysticism is
essentially one by arguing for distinctly plural forms. Chapters 4 and
5 treat those commentators who explain mysticism as a way of life
involving various stages and levels. These authors frequently consider mysticism to be the very summit of human existence and what life
is ultimately all about. Chapters 6 and 7 look at those authors who
have opened up Christian mysticism to the mystical riches of the
Eastern tradition and at those highly critical of this Eastern orientation.

Because mysticism must be evaluated and critically interpreted,
Chapter 8 delineates the creative, new mystical theology of Karl
Rahner, S.J. Finally, since the entire theological approach to mysti-
cism is in need of a solid methodological basis for its contemporary
transposition, the incipient mystical theology of Bernard Lonergan,
S.J. is explained in Chapter 9.

Readers might ask the following questions to guide them
through the maze of positions and counterpositions in this book. Is
mysticism a psychological abnormality or does it lead to human
authenticity? Should one distinguish between a genuine and a pseudo-mysticism? Is mysticism reserved for an elite or is everyone called
to authentic mysticism? Must it be studied from both a scientific and
a religious point of view? What relationship does mysticism have to
the occult and to visions, locutions, the stigmata, levitation, etc.? Are
there irreducible plural forms of mysticism or are its essential function and structure one and the same? Does the mystic's union with
the Absolute dissolve or strengthen his identity? Can mysticism be

reduced to ecstatic moments of rapture or is it more a way of life with stages of purification, illumination, and unification with the Absolute? Does the mystic destroy or purify and enhance the religious tradition out of which she comes? Is the mystic a selfish recluse or a powerful, pragmatic social force? How do mystical experience and interpretation interact? Are there graced mysticisms outside of Christianity? Is experience enough or is the "object" with which the mystic unites the ultimate sanction of the mystical life?

Finally, I would like to thank John Carmody, Sr. Jo-Ann Veillette and Mary Luti for reading the entire manuscript and for their valuable suggestions. And special thanks to my Carmelite sisters in Christ for their prayers for this project and for living in a special way what this book is really all about.

1
Psychological Approaches I

William James

Past psychological studies of mystical phenomena have frequently reflected an unusually strong hostility toward religion. These studies, moreover, often attempted to explain mysticism away by reducing it to deviant behavior, repressed eroticism, madness, mental illness, regression to infantile states, or an escape from the problems of daily life. The older psychology tended to label the great mystics of the Eastern and Western traditions as misfits, deviants, lunatics, and the victims of self-hypnosis and auto-suggestion.

Perhaps no book in this century has done more to render psychology benevolent to mysticism and religion than William James' classic on the psychology of religion, *The Varieties of Religious Experience.*[1] This book has, in fact, influenced to some extent almost every noteworthy contemporary study of mysticism. Some would call James the grandfather of American mystical studies, because he stands at the beginning of the mystical fascination which so dominates contemporary society.

Especially well-known are his four marks of mystical experience: ineffability, noetic quality, transiency, and passivity.[2] Ineffability, for James, means that mysticism must be directly experienced in order to be understood. For example, one needs to have been in love to understand a lover's mind; one must possess a musical ear to appreciate a concert.

Mystical experiences have a noetic quality since they convey states of knowledge. All mystics speak of revelations, illuminations, significance, and meanings which transcend the discursive intellect. Supra-conceptual and trans-rational knowledge stamps the mystic's experiences.

Because these experiences rarely last longer than a few hours, and in most cases much less, James calls them transient. Yet, "mystical states, strictly so called, are never merely interruptive. . . . They modify the inner life of the subject between the times of their recurrence" (pp. 293–94). For James, therefore, genuine mystical experience changes a person.

Finally, no matter what a person does to obtain these experiences, no matter how hard he works, they are always experienced as a gift, as transcending all ascetical preparations. The person feels in the power of something superior, passive, and acted upon instead of acting.

Some commentators have cogently shown, however, that James' marks are wide enough to fit any one of many mutually exclusive experiences.[3] These "marks" may characterize ethical, aesthetic, nature, athletic, and philosophical experiences as well as mystical experiences. In short, they are too broad to be of much use.

To maintain, moreover, the absolute ineffability of mystical experience is a contradiction, as these same commentators point out. All experience is ineffable in the banal sense of not being able to be directly shared or communicated to another. And, as Peter Moore notes, many mystics do take considerable care and subtlety to describe the actual contents of their experiences.[4] For him, "the relationship of the mystic to the non-mystic is not . . . like the relationship of the sighted to the blind, but more like that of the sighted to those with at least a glimmering of sight."[5] The explicit mystic can and does communicate with the implicit mystic in all of us.

James also seems somewhat unaware of the mystical *states* which the mystic lives for a period of time and which transcend his "transiency" category. E. W. Trueman Dicken, for example, has underscored the importance of different stages and states of mystical experience, a point receiving more attention from contemporary scholars.[6]

The mystic's experience of union is mysticism's salient feature, according to James. Union with the Absolute and awareness of this union "is the everlasting and triumphant mystical tradition hardly altered by differences of clime or creed" (p. 321). The mystic considers what he experiences to be somehow ultimate. Moreover, because the mystic in some traditions claims to become the Absolute, James stresses the pantheistic, monistic, optimistic, and conversion traits of mystical consciousness. Since Christians speak of unity, not merging, with a personal God, however, James distinguishes Christian mysticism from a "naturalistic pantheism." The characteristic of unity with the Absolute provides James with the cutting-edge for his clean distinction between genuine mysticism and those phenomena often confused with it, i.e., parapsychology, mystery-mongering, spiritualism, and the occult. The vast majority of contemporary commentators agree with this distinction, moreover.

Concerning the nature of with what the mystic has united, James offers the following hypothesis:

> . . . whatever it may be on its *farther* side, the "more" with which in religious experience we feel ourselves connected is on its *hither* side the subconscious continuation of our conscious life . . . primarily the higher faculties of our own hidden mind which are controlling, the sense of union with the power beyond us is a sense of something, not merely apparently, but literally true (p. 386).

James, therefore, is relatively unconcerned about knowing the exact nature of the goal of the mystical quest. As long as "we can experience union with *something* larger than ourselves, and in that union find our greatest peace . . . anything larger will do" (pp. 395–96).

Mystics of various traditions would maintain, on the other hand, that "something larger" will not always do. Mysticism involves self-emptying; it matters greatly, therefore, with what the mystic allows herself to be filled. Many authors argue for a mysticism of union with the Triune God, with all of nature, with one's own spiritual substance, with angelic and demonic powers, with a variety of archetypes of good and evil, to name but a few. St. John of the Cross teaches, for example, that the soul has various centers.[7]

The mystic, therefore, may unite with a whole variety of realities.[8] For the Judeo-Christian-Islamic tradition, however, only one is holy. And as the mystical tradition unanimously teaches, union with certain powers of evil produces disastrous results.

The extremely dynamic, useful, practical, creative lives of so many of the great mystics impressed the father of American pragmatism. He saw in the life of St. Ignatius of Loyola, for example, "one of the most powerful practical human engines that ever lived" (p. 317). The fruits of the mystics' lives, the great benefits to society which flowed from the great active mystics, proved for James the value of the mystical life.

Christian mystics and theologians would question, however, James' cursory dismissal of St. Margaret Mary, because her life did not meet the standards of American pragmatism and self-actualization. It is too narrow to limit mysticism's worth to the attractive, personal integration and active lifestyle of certain strong mystics. The Christian mystical heritage also reveals those mystics who have been called to incarnate in their lives Christ's passion and shameful death, his social rejection, his failure, his disgrace, his loneliness and isolation on the cross, and his entombment. Mystical "victim souls" participate in Christ's redemptive work and must be discerned with the eyes of faith, as difficult as that discernment may be.

For James, well-developed mystical states bestow upon the mystic a certain "invulnerability," a faith-stance which produces an unshakable way of life. He further claims that these states "usually are, and have the right to be, absolutely authoritative over the individuals to whom they come" (p. 323). On the other hand, he limits the mystic's truth-claims to the mystics themselves. Mystical truth exists for the individual mystic and for no one else, because "no authority emanates from them which should make it a duty for those who stand outside of them to accept their revelations uncritically" (p. 324).

The "more" with which the mystic unites produces a feeling of expansion, freedom, and union. Since it has "no specific intellectual content whatsoever of its own" (p. 326), for James, it may be united with highly different philosophies and theologies, or "over-beliefs." Mystical experiences do not prove the creeds of any particular religion, theology, or philosophy. The mystical experience and the resulting way of life—not the theories—remain central for James. Still, the very existence of mystical states "absolutely overthrows the pretensions of non-mystical states to be the sole and ultimate dictators of what we may believe" (p. 327). James emphatically rejects rational consciousness as the only authority in life and views it as only one possible type of consciousness.

Many studies concur with James that no true propositions can result from mystical experience.[9] For example, although Steven Katz seems to deny that mystical claims are so much "mumbo-jumbo" and refuses to reduce these claims to psychological projections, he asserts that "no veridical propositions can be generated on the basis of mystical experience."[10] Carl Keller bluntly states that "the student of mysticism cannot reach beyond his own personal experience."[11]

This skepticism is by no means universal, however. The profound epistemological studies of Joseph Maréchal, Louis Dupré, Jacques Maritain, and others provide sufficient epistemological grounds for taking the mystics' truth claims seriously.[12] Perhaps the cognitional theory of Bernard Lonergan, S.J., whose work will be examined later, will show that the difficulty of establishing the truth claims of the mystics differs only somewhat from establishing *any* truth claims.

In addition to religious mysticism, James also describes what he calls a "diabolical mysticism." This consists of delusions, paranoia, desolations, pessimism, negative feelings and meanings, "a sort of religious mysticism turned upside down" (p. 326). From the view of Christian theology, however, the question can be raised whether James has confused here two different types of mystical experiences. Mystical purgation, the dark nights of the senses and the spirit, the intense mystical desolations and deaths through which authentic mystics of both the Eastern and the Western mystical tradition have passed as a necessary step toward illumination and union cannot be called "diabolical" without confusing the issue. The mystical tradition has long distinguished authentic purgation from the illnesses, frenzies, degenerate behavior, and excesses resulting from *pseudo*-mysticism.[13]

James would also maintain that religion, morality, contemplation, etc., are not the only means for awakening mystical consciousness. Nature, intoxicants, and anaesthetics may also produce mystical experience. As James says, "the drunken consciousness is one bit of the mystical consciousness" (p. 297). Many commentators agree with James that nature can trigger mystical experience. Many mystics and commentators maintain, on the other hand, that a proper discernment of spirits would reject the drunken consciousness as so much pseudo-mysticism. If James so highly values strength of personality, integrity of life, creativity, social concerns, and pragmatic results as stemming from the mystical consciousness, it is difficult to see how he can accept the drunken consciousness which produces the opposite effects.

Richard Bucke

Many who write about mysticism herald Richard Bucke's *Cosmic Consciousness* as a classic study of the evolution of the human mind.[14] In his book, Bucke describes three differing types of consciousness: simple, self, and cosmic. Animals, says Bucke, possess simple consciousness, or an awareness of their surroundings and their bodies. Self-consciousness belongs to man, for he not only knows his environment but is also conscious of being distinct from it.

Cosmic consciousness is a "higher form of consciousness than that possessed by ordinary man" (p. 1). It is as qualitatively superior to self-consciousness as self-consciousness is to simple consciousness. Cosmic consciousness bestows illuminations about the nature of the universe, a universe now experienced not as a "dead machine" but as a living presence, infinitely good in its essence and finality.

Often coming without warning, cosmic consciousness seems to immerse the person into a flame or rosy cloud. The oneness of all things becomes transparent. Sin is now seen as an illusion, and the fear of death melts away. Personal immortality and the eternal nature of all life seem assured. This experience transforms the person both interiorly and exteriorly. Experiencing joy, salvation, victory, and assurance, the person becomes a new creature with a radiant appearance and an increased ability both to learn and to lead others into what has been given. Perhaps most important of all, the person who passes from self-consciousness to cosmic consciousness knows that "the universe is God and that God is the universe, and that no evil ever did or ever will enter into it" (p. 17).

The one attaining cosmic consciousness is a new creature, the prototype of evolution's attempt to produce a new species. This attainment, for Bucke, is "acquired only by the best specimens of the race but also when they are at their best" (p. 65). Bucke has discovered that this new ability has been called different names throughout the ages: Nirvana, Kingdom of God, Kingdom of Heaven, Christ, Spirit of God, Gabriel, Beatrice, my Soul, Specialism, etc.

History discloses only fourteen "great cases" of cosmic consciousness: the Buddha, Jesus Christ, St. Paul, Plotinus, Mohammed, Dante, Bartolome Las Casas, John Ypes, Francis Bacon, Jacob Behmen, William Blake, Honoré de Balzac, Walt Whitman, and Edward Carpenter. Bucke makes much of their masculinity, intellectual and moral superiority, physical gifts, and their 30–40 year age-level. He also finds in thirty-six others, from Moses to persons whose identity he does not disclose, lesser, imperfect, and doubtful cases of cosmic consciousness.

The manifestations of cosmic consciousness force Bucke to ask a timely question: "[H]ow, then, shall we know that this is a new sense, revealing fact, and not a form of insanity, plunging its subject into delusion" (p. 70)? The heightened moral qualities and self-restraint of those with cosmic consciousness clearly distinguish them from the insane, for Bucke. Much of modern civilization, moreover, "rests . . . very largely on the teaching of the new sense" (p. 70) and that "we have the same evidence of the objective reality which corresponds to this faculty that we have of the reality which tallies any other sense or faculty whatever" (p. 71).

Few contemporary authors, however, agree with Bucke that Jesus, St. Paul, or St. John of the Cross identified God with the universe or that they lost their intense sense of sin and evil. Should one, moreover, really list Walt Whitman or Edward Carpenter, for example, along with Jesus and the Buddha? Are not Ps. Dionysius, St. Teresa of Avila and Johann Arndt, to name a few, as important as some of those listed in the fourteen "great cases"? Few commentators would accept the identification of Nirvana, the Kingdom of God, Gabriel, Christ, Beatrice, etc.

Some commentators, R. C. Zaehner, for one, maintain that Bucke has actually described "nature mysticism." Because the human person is essentially spirit-in-world, with this spirit having an absolutely fundamental relationship to the world, a mystical experience of the unity of all created things is possible, from the perspective of Christian theology. Perhaps the paradigm of the spirit-in-world mystical experience, cosmic consciousness, is the Zen *satori* experience, which has been described as a deep intuition of being and a recognition of the inherent unity of one's own being with the being of everything else.

Deep within the human spirit exists a basic relationship to all things which experientially comes to the fore in *satori*, or cosmic consciousness. Even in less intense forms than *satori*, this spirit-in-world experience shows itself in experiences of nature at sunrise, at sunset, at the ocean, in the mountains, etc., where we feel a close kinship with all created things.

Karl Rahner has written of the human spirit's "pancosmic" relationship with the unity of all things at the moment of death.[15] Perhaps cosmic consciousness, or nature mysticism, or *satori*, is an intense form of the human spirit's pancosmic relationship with all created things which reaches its high point in and through death. Rahner's caution against confusing an experience of the human spirit's oneness with all created things with an authentic God-experience should also be noted.[16]

On the other hand, could cosmic consciousness possibly be an experience of the ground of all created things, an experience of the silent God? Evelyn Underhill may be correct when she assesses cosmic consciousness as only a part or only one aspect of full mystical consciousness.[17]

Bucke's cosmic consciousness contains, perhaps, elements of what Pierre Scheuer, S.J. has called a "natural mysticism." This mysticism flows from the human spirit's ability to grasp itself intuitively, to be present-to-itself, or, as St. Thomas Aquinas holds, to "return-to-self." As Scheuer writes:

> It is in this passage from the discursive processes of reason and of consciousness to the intuitive function that a *"natural" mysticism* is verified. And in the measure that spirit by itself has already acquired an intuitive consciousness of itself, all the other objects which it knew abstractly in its own activity become likewise terms of intuition.[18]

The second-half of Scheuer's quote explains the mystical basis of much poetic activity and perhaps indicates why so many on Bucke's list are poets.

Frequently accompanying natural mysticism, or cosmic consciousness, however, are the "nights of the spirit which are also death and despair,"[19] phenomena well-described by Jacques Maritain. These nights may aid the poet and artist to purify their art, but they may plunge them into "an annihilation in the sensual; magic; insanity; moral or physical suicide."[20] Perhaps the nights given along with cosmic consciousness aid in clarifying the breakdowns of Rimbaud or Nietzsche, and the excesses of Whitman, Jeffries, and others.

Walter T. Stace

The writings of Walter T. Stace have enjoyed wide recognition among scholars of mysticism. He defines mysticism as "the apprehension of *an ultimate nonsensuous unity in all things,* a oneness or a One to which neither the senses nor reason can penetrate" (p. 14).[21] Fully developed mystical experience eliminates all multiplicity and distinctions from consciousness, leaving a pure consciousness beyond subject and object. As Stace repeatedly emphasizes: "The core of the experience is thus described as an undifferentiated unity—a oneness or unity in which there is no internal division, no multiplicity" (p. 20).

Mystical consciousness, for Stace, must be utterly empty and pure. It surpasses all dualism, exhibits a unity without any differences, and rests in absolute unity. "Formless, shapeless, colorless, odorless, soundless" (p. 12), neither sensations, nor thoughts, nor concepts inhabit this ultimate achievement of the human mind.

Stace distinguishes between the extrovertive and the introvertive mystical consciousness. The former experiences unity amidst the things of the world, in a transfigured world unified by something ultimate. The latter involves the voiding of all empirical contents from consciousness to discover the One at the person's deepest center. Stace prefers the latter and judges it to have been the most important in human history.

Having defined the mystical consciousness as essentially formless and as an undifferentiated unity, Stace, like most contemporary commentators, distinguishes mysticism from the occult, spiritualism, and the parapsychological. He rejects mysticism as meaning anything which is misty, foggy, or poetic. He further denies that visions and locutions have anything to do with genuine mysticism, conceding, however, that some mystics do experience these. In addition, for Stace, there is nothing essentially religious about an undifferentiated unity experience. Its formlessness, the experience of somehow melting into infinity, the emotional overtones—all of these help to transpose the mystical experience into a great variety of religious forms. Yet, for Stace, mysticism's "connection with religion is subsequent and even adventitious" (p. 23). Plotinus illustrates this and the Buddha shows that mysticism and atheism can coexist, according to Stace.

The undifferentiated unity stance contradicts, of course, the Judeo-Christian-Islamic claim that becoming God or merging with Him in some way is impossible. Orthodox Christian mysticism stresses a differentiated unity with God, or becoming God by participation while retaining one's own identity. Jewish mysticism holds for a possible "adhesion" to God, something which Stace rejects as "not what is meant by mysticism elsewhere" (p. 222). Stace further contends that union with God is not possible, for union must bring about identity.

Since all fully developed mystical experience, for Stace, is undifferentiated unity, he locates the decisive difference among the mystics of various religious traditions solely in the way they have interpreted their experiences. As he says, "each culture and each religion interprets this undifferentiated unity in terms of its own creeds or dogmas" (p. 21). This means that Christian mystics in reality experience an undifferentiated unity, but redogmatize this in terms of differentiated unity because of theological and ecclesiastical pressure.

This sharp distinction between experience and interpretation underpins Stace's bias. He praises the pantheistic interpretation of mystical experience as being "not only natural but constitut[ing] the more perfect type of mysticism, while the dualistic interpretation—as expressed, for example, by Ruysbroeck and St. John of the Cross—is relatively underdeveloped" (p. 202). Stace asserts, moreover, that neither Jesus nor St. Paul was a mystic. On the other hand, the bold statement of pantheism, "I am God," makes him uneasy. "The truth," says Stace, "if expressed in theistic language, is not simply identity with God but rather unity in difference" (p. 202).

Despite Christianity's interpretative and speculative inferiority, Stace highly values its emphasis upon love of God and neighbor. In fact, Christianity's focus upon love "is especially characteristic of Christian mysticism to such an extent that this alone is sufficient to distinguish it from all other mysticisms" (p. 130).

Stace repudiates the notion that the mystic is a selfish introvert. Self-sacrifice, service, charity, mercy, and many other practical deeds flow from the mystical life. In fact, for Stace, "mysticism is the source from which ethical values ultimately flow" (p. 26). Its power to transform the individual and human life in general testifies to its incomparable value.

Finally, Stace stresses the mystic's experiential excellence, not his philosophy or theology. Still, he seems to reject the position that mysticism is a purely subjective experience. "Mystical experience," he writes, "is in touch with that cosmic Spiritual Presence toward which the great world religions all dimly grope" (p. 236).

Many commentators, on the other hand, deny that the somewhat overworked distinction between experience and interpretation does sufficient justice to the great variety of mystical experiences and traditions. Steven Katz, for example, contends that "there are no pure (i.e., unmediated) experiences."[22] Stace's post-experiential interpretative theory overlooks the mystic's pre-mystical consciousness which "is at work before, during, and after the experience."[23]

The works of Annemarie Schimmel, Robert Ellwood, and Geoffrey Parrinder also emphasize the mystic's total spiritual and social environment.[24] Other writers agree with Katz, moreover, that "mystical experience is 'over-determined' by its socio-religious milieu"[25] and that "beliefs shape experience, just as experience shapes belief."[26] The mystic's beliefs, intentions, motivations, contemplative techniques, spiritual director; the object of her quest; her entire conceptual, social, historical, linguistic matrix—in short, her entire formative milieu significantly affects and effects the experience itself, not merely its interpretation after the fact.

Peter G. Moore, among others, questions Stace's reduction of all mystical experience to the experience of undifferentiated unity. "It is doubtful," writes Moore, "whether his arguments are based upon a sufficiently accurate phenomenology of mystical experience."[27] A phenomenology of the love mysticisms found, for example, in Christian bridal mysticism or the Hindu *bhakti* tradition gives sufficient evidence for a differentiated unity experience wherein two become one and yet remain two. Moore also points out that Stace neglects the highly important lower stages of mysticism to focus exclusively upon its highest stage which in Stace's case may be only a fictional "philosophical abstraction."

Although Stace appeals to St. John of the Cross to exclude visions and locutions from genuine mysticism, St. John of the Cross never denied the God-given, mystical quality of some of these phenomena. He taught instead that they can be safely rejected by the mystic because their main effect is instantaneous. Recent commentators, moreover, tend to distinguish far less sharply than past commentators a so-called mystical essence from visions, locutions, and other mystical phenomena.[28] Peter Moore argues, moreover, that it makes no more sense to exclude these phenomena from a philosophical study of mysticism than it would to exclude dreams from a study of human psychology just because many people consider dreams insignificant.[29]

Finally, although many commentators agree that not all mysticism needs to be religious and that a type of mysticism can be cultivated outside of a religious context, Stace's contention that mysticism's connection with religion is subsequent and even adventitious does not stand. Georges Morel, Robert Ellwood, and Annemarie Schimmel, to name but a few, have cogently shown the intrinsic connection between mysticism and religion.[30] In fact, there is a sense in which all great religions are mystical at heart and that mysticism is the full-flowering of any religious tradition.

Summary

Despite the fact that some commentators now consider James, Bucke, and Stace to be somewhat passé, contemporary books on mysticism still continue to build upon their foundations. James' four marks of ineffability, noetic quality, passivity, and transiency have gained wide acceptance and have produced creative counterpositions, as we have seen. James' emphasis upon union as the hallmark of mysticism is now a firmly established position, although many reject his relative indifference to that with which the mystic unites himself.

James, Bucke, and Stace distinguish genuine mysticism from insanity and the occult; moreover, they all emphasize the life-enhancing features of the mystical consciousness. While James distinguishes nature from theistic mysticism, Bucke and Stace maintain that mysticism is one and the same the world over. Authors treated later on, such as Smart, Huxley, Fischer, Hocking, Underhill, and Wapnick, agree with Bucke and Stace. On the other hand, those arguing for irreducibly plural forms of mystical experience are Zaehner, Rahner, Maritain, Maréchal, O'Brien, and others. Whereas Stace insists upon the undifferentiated unity quality of all mystical experience, others insist as strongly that union with a difference characterizes many mystical traditions.

Stace's strong distinction between experience and its interpretation has provoked the counterposition which stresses how deeply interpretation itself enters into an experience and how important the formative milieu is for actual mystical experience. Finally, James, Bucke, and Stace reject the face-value truth-claims of mystical statements, but do not reduce them to projections of psychological experience.

The next section focuses upon contemporary authors whose psychological perspective is perhaps more empirical than the above, but in some ways more limited, as we shall see.

2
Psychological Approaches II

Erich Neumann

One finds in the penetrating work of Erich Neumann a paradigm of contemporary Jungian approaches to mystical studies. For him, the human person is intrinsically mystical, *homo mysticus.* He focuses upon mystical anthropology, because he sees the human person in a continuous process of transformation resulting from a mystical interaction between ego, consciousness, and the unconscious. Consciousness is born out of the primordial womb of the unconscious, that omnipresent, unchanging, and everywhere identical substrate of the psyche in its individual and collective aspects. The ego is the center of consciousness. For Neumann, "the personality is constantly changed from its own center outward, by the spontaneous action of the creative unconscious" (p. 377).[1] This interaction between the ego and the unconscious is essentially mystical.

Individual and collective human progress goes from the "uroboros state," a fetal state, a state of undifferentiated consciousness or primal chaos in which the ego and consciousness have still to develop, to a state of consciousness and individuality whose center is the ego. Paradoxically, the unconscious both promotes and strives to prevent this growth in clarity, consciousness, differentiation, and responsible awareness.

In order to progress, the ego must frequently renounce conscious reality and descend into the unconscious to meet an essentially numinous non-ego. As Neumann says, "the encounter with the numinous constitutes the 'other side' of the development of consciousness and is by nature 'mystical' " (p. 380). Also, "for us the mystical is rather a fundamental category of human experience which, psychologically speaking, manifests itself wherever consciousness is not yet, or is no longer, effectively centered around the ego" (p. 378).

The ego must surrender to the unconscious, to an "area of nothingness" to experience "the creative void" (p. 383), but without relinquishing its identity or slackening the tension between itself and the unconscious. The Jungians call the center of the creative void the self. It is the central archetype, cannot be empirically distinguished from the God-image, and represents the totality of personality. It surpasses the ego, is both the center and circumference of consciousness and the unconscious, and is our life's goal. "The self," writes Neumann, "is associated with the archetypal perfection situation of the uroboros as the source situation of the isolated ego-existence" (p. 385). Because the self is both transpersonal and the center of personality, as the personality begins to individuate, it experiences itself as ego-self, something which is intimate enough to be me but great enough to be God.

Within that framework, Neumann distinguishes between early, high, and ultimate levels of mysticism. This triad refers "both to the stages of human development, in the course of which ego-consciousness arose, and to the stages in the life of the individual, which, in broad outlines at least, recapitulates the phylogenetic development" (p. 389). Primitive man and children experience early mysticism, which is essentially a mysticism of source and origin, dominated by the archetypes of uroboros and the Great Mother, symbols of an all-embracing unconscious. Because the ego has not completely separated from the non-ego at this stage, the person readily experiences the numinous archetypes of the transpersonal world. Levy-Bruhl has called this a *participation mystique.*

Ego and consciousness, moreover, mean pain, conflict, division, and distinctions. A relatively weak, undeveloped, germinal ego, therefore, craves "uroboros incest," a return to the conditions prior to the division between unconsciousness and ego. Should the person work to kill the ego in mystical dissolution by rejecting ego, consciousness, world, and humanity, Neumann labels this "nihilistic uroboros mysticism" (pp. 398f.). This anticosmic mysticism fixates the person in the uroboros prenatal state and leads to disintegration, regression, and nihilism. Instead of striving to integrate the world of contradictions, the pathological, unstable, primitive ego surrenders even the inferiority of its consciousness to the terrible "devouring Mother." Seizure, ecstasy, inflation, and depression mark this low-level mysticism. Neumann also calls it "somnambulistic" (p. 388).

For Neumann, however, "it is in the very nature of the creative principle to progress from an uroboros world system without ego or consciousness, to a cosmos anthropocentrically ordered round the ego-consciousness" (p. 398). Hence, should the ego return from the unconscious, strengthened and creative, to the sphere of human life with a positive attitude toward the world, after passing through the various stages of mystical introversion, this is "immanent world-transforming mysticism" (pp. 397f.).

At psychological puberty, the ego conquers the terrible aspects of the unconscious and separates from its cosmic parents. It must now fight the dragon, undergo rebirth and transformation to acquire higher manhood and emerge as the "heroic ego." Love and rebirth mysticisms, for Neumann, characterize this stage as "dragon-fight mysticism" (p. 400). The person accepts life in the world as creative and withstands the heightened tension between the ego and the self. The ego unites with the "higher man" and emerges as the "hero," the "great individual," like unto God. This is essentially a mysticism of vocation, mission, and world-transformation.

Neumann views the ecstatic mysticism of Yoga, Buddhism, St. Teresa of Avila, St. John of the Cross, etc., not as an uroboros mysticism, but as the zenith of hero-mysticism. Their plunge into the creative void led not to a drunken disintegration, but to a reinforcement of the ego through extreme exertion. Asceticism and strict ethical attitudes prepared the way for the transformation of their consciousness. The ego renounced its autonomy and the self became the center of the new personality. As Neumann says, "the ego must increase its charge of energy in order to make possible its own suspension and transposition" (p. 404).

The final and mature phase of mysticism, for Neumann, centers upon Jungian individuation, self-realization, the transformation into the self, the person's ultimate wholeness and uniqueness. Neumann's self is both prepsychological and extrapsychological; it is, moreover, "extrahuman, superhuman, and divine, but ... must also be said to constitute the human as such" (p. 413). The self does not coincide with the unconscious, but with the God-image, from which it cannot be empirically distinguished.

The mature mystic has synthesized his encounters with his numinous depths and his concrete situation in the given world so well as to be a center of new life. Personal transformation and heightened creative activity in the world mark this stage. Both the self and the world become transparent where "man and godhead meet one another in the open" (p. 414). The mature mystic has successfully resisted the temptation to dissolve his identity in this transparency. Heaven and earth, moreover, seem to merge, and the mystic discovers eternal life hidden in this world. An afterlife in the strict sense is, therefore, unnecessary.

Neumann argues for a great variety of mystical experiences: theistic, pantheistic, panentheistic, materialistic, idealistic, extraverted, introverted, personal, and transpersonal. What they all have in common, however, is the psychological experience of numinous elements threatening the ego's conscious life. It would seem, therefore, that the great variety and quality of archetypes, or psychic possibilities, which are part of the inherited structure of the psyche, might explain shamanistic experiences, the world of Carlos Casteneda, and psychedelic drug experiences.[2] For Neumann, however, the supreme form of mysticism preserves the greatest tension between the ego and the self.[3]

Mystical experience is, for Neumann, intrinsically heretical, anti-dogmatic, anti-collective, and in opposition to the dominant, conscious contents of "the cultural canon." Peter Moore, on the other hand, is paradigmatic of those scholars who hold the counter-position. He writes:

> In fact the mystics of a particular tradition show no more of a tendency to heterodoxy than do the non-mystics within that tradition. Indeed mystics are often notable for their defense of tradition against heterodox beliefs and practices. It is, however, implausible to suppose that mystics of any

tradition should find their experiences incompatible with the doctrines of the institution in which their experiences have been cultivated.[4]

Mysticism which agrees, therefore, with the traditions out of which it springs cannot be dismissed as "low-level," "disguised," or "redogmatized," as Neumann contends. The genuine mystics of any great religious tradition purify that tradition by experiencing its deepest values and criticizing the deformities. Despite the conflicts which have historically risen between mystics and those in authority, many contemporary scholars agree that religious authorities have both supported and suppressed mystical movements.

The Judeo-Christian-Islamic traditions cannot accept the Jungian tendency to reduce religious realities to "projections of experience that occurs in the psychological inwardness of the *anthropos*" (p. 376).[5] Neumann states, for example, that the Christian doctrine of the Fall is a "fallacy based upon a false historical projection of this archetype [uroboros]" (p. 378). Despite their claims to remain only psychological, Jungians do make many metaphysical statements.

Martin Buber, for one, has challenged the Jungian assertion that God is only an "autonomous psychic content,"[6] a state of soul, and that "God does not exist for Himself."[7] Along with Buber, many would object to the Jungian identification of the self and the God-image. The Christian tradition has long distinguished between contemplation of the image of God and of God Himself. From the *Cloud of Unknowing*, God may be the mystic's being, but the mystic is not God's being.

Another noted Jungian, Ira Progoff, further exemplifies the Jungian tendency to reduce even salvation history to psychic inwardness. For him, "each human soul contains a Bible within itself. . . . Perhaps there are . . . many new Bibles to be created as the sign of spiritual unfoldment among many persons in the modern era."[8] It might be argued that the human psyche, however, finds the reality of its desires fulfilled in salvation history. The psyche's a priori possibilities, the purely formal, devoid-of-content, archetypes may actually find their true content in the realities of Judeo-Christian salvation history. From the perspective of Christian theology, it is here that the ideal correspondence between psyche and salvation history is to be found. But it is in the canon of Christian Scripture that the norm for the correct correspondence between psyche and its concrete expression is to be sought.

Miscellaneous Psychological Approaches

At this point, a brief presentation of a sample of the vast, often-bewildering, psychological explanations of mystical phenomena seems appropriate. John White, for example, reduces the great variety, depth, and quality of mystical phenomena to a common denominator when he labels St. Paul's "peace that surpasses understanding," Bucke's "cosmic consciousness," Maslow's "peak experience," Jung's "individuation," etc., as the "highest state of consciousness."[9] He places, moreover, Jesus, the Buddha, Walt Whitman, and Aldous Huxley on the same level of human achievement, compassion, and creativity.

Mysticism, for White, returns a person to a primal state. In this state, the person regains a primitive condition in supraconsciousness. "By recovering his animal nature, man becomes God,"[10] he writes. Assuming that all mystical experiences are the same and monistic, White lists the "classic trigger situations": fasting, self-torture, extreme fatigue, sexual relations, dance, prayer, yoga, Zen, hypnosis, occult methods, electric shock, etc. White seems, moreover, to consider consciousness and God equivalents. He writes: "[R]eturn to the godhead (content of consciousness) is equivalent with awareness of Cosmic Awareness (consciousness itself)."[11]

Raymond Prince and Charles Savage focus upon the therapeutic value of regression, or returning to earlier levels of functioning. For them, regression and creativity go hand-in-hand. More to the point, for these psychologists, "the hypothesis is that mystical states represent regression in the service of the ego."[12] The mystic's world-denying attitude and activities, moreover, aid the regression to the earliest nursing experiences, or the pleasurable fusion with the nursing mother.

Alexander Maven suggests still another reduction of mysticism to biology. During mystical experience, for Maven, the mystic allegedly "remembers" his father's sperm penetrating, being absorbed by, and dissolving into his mother's ovum. He offers, therefore, "the possibility that the experience of mystic union in its various forms may be a 'playback' of a record of the mystic's biological conception, as it might have been experienced, respectively, by the ovum, the sperm, and by both together."[13]

In contrast to these tendencies to reduce mysticism to biology and regression, Claire Owens emphasizes that only superficial similarities exist between the mystical state, the infantile state, and the psychotic state. In Jungian fashion, she underscores mysticism as the natural tendency of the unconscious toward personal wholeness. She writes: "The mystical, psychotic, and infant states will continue to be confused until we are willing to accept the fact that the contents of the unconscious are multiplex, and that oversimplifications made for the purpose of easy categorization are premature."[14] She does accept, however, the Jungian idea that psychic energy regresses into the deepest regions of the collective unconscious, "the matrix of his own identity as well as the source of his humanity,"[15] but in order to help the person progress in creativity, integrity, and individuation. Owens, moreover, seems to agree with Neumann that both ends of the consciousness spectrum must be examined in mystical considerations. Low-level mysticism leads to the dissolution of consciousness. The Christian tradition has called this "pseudo-mysticism." High-level mysticism intensifies consciousness and heightens awareness. For example, sniffing glue produces a state of consciousness at the oppposite end of the consciousness spectrum from that produced by yogic meditation.

Kenneth Wapnick describes mysticism as a healthy form of schizophrenia. The person plunges into the inner world to return, at will, refreshed, recreated, and transformed.[16] The mystic, unlike the pathological schizophrenic, however, has learned to synthesize the often contradictory elements of the inner and outer life. Along these same lines, R. D. Laing views the mystic as a healthy madman who protests the insanities of life. "Madness need not be all breakdown. It may also be breakthrough,"[17] he writes.

The human person, in Roland Fisher's view, is essentially a sensory computer which collects and processes data. If the processing cannot keep pace with an increasing input, a "jammed computer"[18] state arises, a state he calls mystical. "At the peak of ecstatic states," he writes, "interpretative activity ceases, or . . . there is no data content from without . . . the only content of the experience at the height of rapture being the reflection of the mystic in his own 'program.' "[19]

Arthur Deikman hypothesizes that mystical phenomena occur through a "deautomatization of the psychological structures that organize, limit, select, and interpret perceptual stimuli."[20] Renunciation, asceticism, meditation, etc., break down the ego's normal way of structuring incoming data. The abeyance of ordinary consciousness is not regressive and is characterized by: feelings of intense realness, because images and thoughts seem real; unusual sensations, because normally unconscious intrapsychic processes reach the conscious threshold; the experience of unity which may result from one's own psychic structure or even from the real structure of the world; ineffability; finally, trans-sensate phenomena. With some of the authors considered in Chapter 1, Deikman denies the "epistemological validity"[21] of mystical experiences. They say nothing about reality. The feelings of awe, reverence, beauty, humility, etc., moreover, are more important for Deikman than what ultimately gives rise to these feelings.

Abraham Maslow coined the phrase "peak experiences" for those happy, ecstatic unusual moments of rapture triggered by music, art, scientific discovery, love, friendship, giving birth, prayer, nature, etc., which promote "self-actualization."[22] People feel most themselves during peak experiences. They are self-validating and seem to transcend or to reconcile contradictions and evil. They produce feelings of awe, humility, reverence, surrender, love, and compassion. The person's consciousness becomes egoless, non-clinging, and god-like. And, for Maslow, these experiences are always good.

Some commentators, as we shall see, point out, however, that *some* mystical experiences may be peak, but not all peak experiences are mystical. Peak nature, athletic, and aesthetic experiences, for example, are not mystical. Mystical experiences, moreover, may be dark, silent, and reveal a person's poverty and nakedness. Furthermore, not all mystical *states* and permanent transformations of consciousness are peak in Maslow's sense. Christian mystics are seeking God, not experiences of self-actualization.

Carl Albrecht

There may be no better way to conclude this section than by focusing upon the undeservedly neglected studies of the remarkable German physician, psychologist, and philosopher, Carl Albrecht.[23] Despite his nearly impossible German, Albrecht's critical, attentive, painfully exacting analysis of mystical phenomena merits wider study and recognition.

Reason, according to Albrecht, can neither directly nor completely grasp the essence of mystical phenomena. Like a spiral coiling around ever-more tightly in ever-smaller circles around its center, Albrecht employs what he calls a "negative phenomenology" to separate mysticism's core from all it is not.

First of all, mysticism cannot be reduced to private, intrapsychic processes. Second, it has nothing to do with pathological disorders, madness, or regression. In fact, Albrecht emphasizes the incredibly healing, integrating, and psychosynthetic values of the mystical consciousness. Third, he clearly distinguishes mysticism from the occult, parapsychology, and the experiences of so-called "higher-worlds." He rejects this as pseudo-mysticism. Finally, he refuses to equate mysticism with ecstasy and union. Although commentators have not reached unanimity on these points, the majority of them support Albecht's position.

His negative phenomenology centers upon the "contemplative consciousness," the *Versunkenheitsbewusstsein.* Contemplation detaches consciousness from its surroundings, empties it of its contents, and progressively unifies it. The controlling and directing functions of the "I" disappear, discrete will acts vanish, and the person's entire being seems to be opened and readied. Extensive calm and clarity penetrate all levels of the psyche. "Total experience" characterizes the radical calm and the clear emptiness of the contemplative consciousness. Nothing of the person appears to be left out of a deep, underlying unity. For Albrecht, the contemplative consciousness is the highest level of human consciousness possible.

Albrecht defines mysticism in the strict sense as the "arrival," the *Ankunft,* in contemplation of an "embracing-Something," an *Umfassendes.* Both the "arrival" of this "embracing-Something" and the ecstatic experience of it are mystical. The person may experience either an "approaching-Something," an *Ankommendes,* as mystical or effected by a mystical "it."

Negative phenomenology can distinguish the "embracing-Something" of mystical experience from elements which arise from the self. Albrecht always sharply distinguishes the subject of mystical experience from its object. He emphasizes that the "approaching, embracing-Something" comes neither from the unconscious nor from the self, but from an unknown source. The contemplative consciousness experiences in unclear certainty a personal or an impersonal "embracing Someone or Something" from a totally foreign sphere.

Mysticism, for Albrecht, contradicts all attempts to ground it anthropologically as a structure of being-in-the-world. He represents a counterpoint to Neumann's mystical man, because for Albrecht human existence is clearly being-in-the-world with a non-worldly reference. For him, mysticism highlights the other-worldly, supra-worldly, character of human existence.

The arrival of a presence, an other, otherness, the not-I, an exclusive object in sharp contrast to the contemplative "I," characterizes the mystical experience. Encounter, communion, communication, dialogue, an entrusting to a non-subjective, hidden presence, predominate. To be, for Albrecht, is to be encountered. The "I" perdures, therefore, throughout the mystical experience. On the other hand, the "I" of the contemplative state is not the familiar, daily "I." To be sure, this "I" can be lost during mystical ecstasy, but not all mystical experience is ecstatic. Nor are all ecstatic experiences, for Albrecht, mystical.

The contemplative consciousness, the condition of "approaching," and the "embracing-Something" constitute the elements of what Albrecht calls a mystical "relation." The mystical "relation" occurs between an inner vision sometimes produced during contemplative consciousness and the "approaching, embracing-Something." It is in this sense that mysticism, for Albrecht, is the "between" of a mysterious presence.

The mystical "relation" is very important because it banishes all critical doubt, cannot be reduced to anything else, and, for Albrecht, is a "phenomenological ultimate." Because it is absolutely deception-free, it is the bedrock of mystical experience.

The contemplative consciousness may encounter filmstrip-like experience, intensified hidden feelings becoming manifest, metaphors, symbols, somatic attacks, self-understanding, and locutions. Albrecht notes the qualitative difference of these "arriving-Somethings" and emphasizes the importance of the mystical locutions. The underlying unity and possible union between the contemplative subject and the mystical object may incarnate itself in speech which is neither the actual mystic's self-expression nor only a signal of mystical presence. The mystical word expresses, incarnates, re-presents what is taking place between both.

Albrecht gives various examples of these primal mystical words which are spoken during contemplation. They are always clear and pregnant with meaning, in contrast with other events taking place in the contemplative consciousness. The whole structure of the personality in its relation to mystery seems to speak out in an unmediated, perfectly exposed, holding-nothing-back way. Unlike thoughts which the "I" frequently "has," these mystical words are total experience as knowing. They transcend psychology, for they seem to express the person's basic act of existence.

Contemplation unifies and integrates consciousness in an all-embracing way, and, hence, is psychotherapeutic. The deeper the contemplation, the more integral the consciousness, and the more likely the repressed elements, splinters of the psyche, etc., can arise, be seen in great clarity, and dismissed in a healing, transforming fashion.

Albrecht has studied mystical visions which arise in contemplation. They do not lend themselves to psychoanalysis, because they do not express the disintegrated self. Because these visions express the self's essential relationship to mystery, they are psychosynthetic. Although these visions combine an experience of presence with an image, the experience of presence predominates over any content the images might have. Image is to presence as figure is to ground in a silhouette. In fact, as the content of the mystical vision decreases, the quality of the sense of presence increases. The less the vision-content, the greater the certainty of the genuineness of the mystical experience. For Albrecht, the imageless vision is the ideal. From the gnoseological point of view, it is mysticism's core phenomenon. It points to a naked presence, an unknown, and an unknowable.

Imageless vision is a looking into the darkness in which nothing can be recognized. In the darkness, however, is a presence which the mystic seeks. It is a vision in the darkness, not a vision of darkness. Nothing is seen, but it is not a vision of nothing. It is essentially a radical experience of presence with clarity out of the depths of peace.

Paradoxically, a trans-sensual, trans-occult mystical light is the condition of possibility for vision into darkness. This mystical light provides the horizon in which all images are seen. As the mystical light becomes stronger and purer, the content of any image decreases, giving rise to an even more intense experience of the presence of an "embracing-Something." In this mystical light, the entire world may perhaps become "transparent" and reveal the presence of this "embracing-Something." For Albrecht, this is genuine cosmic consciousness.

Albrecht emphasizes both mystical experience and mystical cognition as a given and a certitude which philosophy and the natural sciences cannot dismiss from their purviews. Mystical cognition is the rationally structured peaking of a wide, non-differentiated field of experience firmly grounded in the mystical relation as a phenomenological ultimate. To be sure, what can be determined psychologically, phenomenologically, and gnoseologically remains only a small part of the mystical experience. Its real depth and fullness, its religious determination, remain undisturbed. Although mysticism, for Albrecht, can be phenomenologically ensured and explained as a natural, healthy, and normal experience, it is not only a natural phenomenon. It demands of its very nature religious and theological meaning.

Summary

This section has centered upon authors like Prince, Savage, and Maven who reduce mysticism to biologism and infantile regression. Neumann, Owens, and Albrecht represent the counterposition. Mysticism is a phenomenological ultimate which cannot be reduced to anything else. Authors such as Prince, Savage, Owens, Wapnick, Neumann, Laing, Deikman, Maslow, and Albrecht affirm the personal integration often resulting from mystical experience.

Deikman's "deautomatization" theory seems to hold some promise for explaining certain aspects of the traditional dark nights of the senses and the spirit. He also defends the position that

statements made on the basis of mystical experience have no epistemological validity.

Unlike Maslow and others still to be considered, Albrecht does
not equate the mystical and the ecstatic. Unlike many commentators,
he also contends that the "I" perdures during mystical experience,
although greatly transformed. He, Owens, and Neumann distinguish
levels of mysticism and pseudo-mysticism, depending upon the integrity and strength of consciousness attained.

Among the above, Albrecht stands alone in defending the radically trans-worldly character of mystical experience. In contrast to
Stace, Neumann, and others, he denies that scientific reason can fully
explain mysticism. It demands of its very nature a religious and
theological interpretation, even when studied from its natural, psychological foundations.

Moore represents the counterposition to Neumann that the
mystic is always heretical and an iconoclast. Buber is paradigmatic of
those commentators who reject the stance taken by Neumann that
religious realities are basically psychological projections. The Jungians, moreover, have forced commentators, especially those in the
Judeo-Christian tradition, to examine more closely the relationship
between salvation history and the structure of the human psyche.

As we have seen, some of the commentators in the first two
chapters contend that all mysticism is essentially the same and an
experience of undifferentiated unity. The next chapter provides a
strong counterpoint to this position.

3

Irreducibly Plural Types
of Mysticisms

R. C. Zaehner

R. C. Zaehner moved from his initial research work in Zoroastrianism to works on mysticism in large part as a reaction to Aldous Huxley's influential book, *The Doors of Perception.*[1] Zaehner wrote his groundbreaking, highly controversial, *Mysticism Sacred and Profane*[2] for two specific reasons. First of all, he wished to counter Huxley's contention that religious, mystical experiences can be produced by ingesting psychedelic drugs. Secondly, he wanted to oppose the *philosophia perennis* thesis of Huxley and others that all mystical experiences are the same and that even their descriptions reflect an underlying similarity which surpasses religious and cultural diversity.[3] For Zaehner, however, all mystics do not speak the same language nor convey the same message, not even within one particular religious tradition. The thesis that all mysticism is one and the same is simply an unsubstantiated assertion which too easily overlooks important differences.

Zaehner strongly rejects Huxley's call for the sacramentalization of psychedelic drugs to make them part of all religions. For Huxley, the desire to escape from the daily ego and one's surroundings is at the root of all religions, a position Zaehner denies. More to the point, Zaehner accuses Huxley of arbitrarily selecting from the mystical writings, of incorrectly interpreting contemplation, and of naively imposing the richly mystical terminology of the Eastern and Western traditions upon his own psychedelic experiences. According to Huxley's criteria, moreover, it is virtually impossible to distinguish psychotic, schizophrenic, and manic-depressive experience from that of genuine mystical experience.[4] Both an adequate phenomenology of mystical experience and the heroic sanctity of the genuine mystic, according to Zaehner, destroy Huxley's identification of mystical and psychedelic experience.

The thesis for which Zaehner is perhaps best known is the following:

> ... there appear to be at least three distinct mystical states which cannot be identical—the pan-en-henic where all creaturely existence is experienced as one and one as all; the state of pure isolation of what we may now call the uncreated soul or spirit from all that is other than itself; and thirdly, the simultaneous loss of the purely human personality, the "ego," and the absorption of the uncreated spirit, the "self," into the essence of God, in Whom both the individual personality and the whole objective world seem to be entirely obliterated (p. 168).

He argues, therefore, for *"at least three* distinct mystical states." In fact, he subtitled his *Mysticism Sacred and Profane* "an inquiry into *some varieties* of praeternatural experience." One could not ask for a more blunt counterpoint to the position that all mystical experiences are essentially the same.

The pan-en-henic mystic experiences Nature in all things and all things as somehow being one in their depth. Because this mystic senses his unity with all creation, he is, perhaps, for Zaehner, all too prone to identify Nature with God. Pan-en-henism, or all-one-ism, therefore, is frequently pantheistic. During this experience, moreover, the mystic reverts to the state which Adam enjoyed in his original innocence before his ego and the unconscious were differentiated.

In Jungian terms, Zaehner identifies this type of mysticism as a descent into the collective unconscious, "namely a consciousness that precedes individuality and which may therefore be regarded as either prenatal or as that consciousness which is generically present in man" (p. 193). For Zaehner, this is also what Bucke means by

"Cosmic Consciousness," James by the "subliminal and transmarginal region," and Huxley by "Mind at large." What is significant in this experience, for Zaehner, is the mystic's sense of having transcended space and time, of feeling that death is somehow unreal, that the within and without of reality are the same, that man really is a microcosm of the macrocosm.

Zaehner also identifies nature mysticism with the manic state of a manic-depressive psychosis. The collective unconscious surges into consciousness, swamps reason, and temporarily takes control. Jungian "positive inflation" results, the mystic experiences union with Nature or something total, and the state is somehow beyond good and evil.

Zaehner finds in the lives of Arthur Rimbaud, Richard Jeffries, and John Custance a confirmation of his thesis that nature mysticism is closely allied with lunacy. Jeffries, for example, seems to have experienced the depressive side of the manic-depressive state, a disintegration of things instead of their unity, the feeling that all will not be well. This is William James' "diabolical mysticism," a mysticism in which the dark side of the collective unconscious takes over and results in "negative inflation." Arthur Rimbaud sought the dissolution of consciousness and flight into the unconscious by way of debauchery, perversion, and drugs. Zaehner says of him: "Perhaps alone among 'nature' mystics Rimbaud rejected the natural mystical experience as a 'lie' " (p. 83).

Nature mysticism, however, may take a much different direction. Zaehner stresses that this mysticism may lead to Jungian "individuation," or the mystic's total personal integration. The psyche's masculine and feminine principles conjoin; the personal and collective unconscious are reconciled with the conscious mind; the person's center of gravity shifts from the ego (the center of conscious life) to the self (the center of psychic and personal wholeness). For Zaehner, "this . . . is as far as purely natural mysticism and 'natural' psychology can take us" (p. 118).

Zaehner sees our psyche tending into two different directions. The first is toward submersion into the unconscious to merge with a larger whole, as shown above. The second is toward pride and self-isolation and involves the pure isolation of the human spirit from all that is not itself. The latter finds fulfillment in a well-known Hindu mysticism.

Samkhya yoga is this mysticism's paradigm, for Zaehner. It aims at separating the spirit from "Nature," which Zaehner identifies with Jung's collective unconscious, "the sum-total of the phenomenal universe and the life-force that keeps it in being" (p. 99). By withdrawing the spirit from all psycho-physical adjuncts, the human spirit *en*statically contemplates itself in itself. Zaehner calls this "downward transcendence," "solipsism," and the reverse of Jungian individuation.

For Zaehner, moreover, the Christian mystic Ruysbroeck recognized this as the soul's natural rest in itself with no love for God. It is also "what Catholics mean by Limbo. It is the highest happiness that man can attain to in isolation from God" (p. 99). Because the mystic experiences his own spirit as the absolute, he expresses it monistically. The monist is left "standing on a peak,"[5] however, having gone as far as possible through human effort. For Zaehner, it is "the necessary step before the 'self' in Jung's sense can enter into direct relationship with God whose existence the monist is forced to deny" (p. 165).

Although Steven Katz might agree with Zaehner that mystical experiences are not essentially one, he argues, on the other hand, that yogic techniques do not produce a type of pure consciousness. Yogic techniques recondition, not uncondition or decondition it. Human consciousness is always, for Katz, a conditioned-contextual consciousness. "This means that the mystic *even* in his state of reconditioned consciousness is also a shaper of his experience."[6]

For Zaehner, therefore, some mystics never get beyond an experience of their own spirit. To support this position, he stresses the distinction made by Richard of St. Victor between "the contemplation of self as the image of God and the contemplation of God himself."[7]

From the perspective of a Jewish mysticism which emphasizes the highly personal "I-Thou"[8] quality of the mystical experience, Martin Buber makes a similar distinction between an experience of the self and an experience of God. He writes:

> Now from my own unforgettable experience I know well
> that there is a state in which the bonds of the personal
> nature of life seem to have fallen away from us and we
> experience an undivided unity. But I do not know—what

the soul willingly imagines (mine too once did it)—that in
this I had attained to a union with a primal being or the
godhead. This is an exaggeration no longer permitted to the
responsible understanding. Responsibly ... I can elicit
from those experiences only that I reached an undifferentiated unity of myself without form or content. I may call
this an original prebiographical unity and suppose that it is
hidden unchanged beneath all biographical change, all development and complication of the soul ... this unity is
nothing but the unity of this soul of mine.[9]

Buber argues from his own experience, therefore, for the existence of
a "pre-biographical unity" of spirit which supports and subsists
beneath all biographical change, a position similar to Zaehner's
views on samkhya yoga.

Zaehner provides many examples from Hinduism, Islam, and
Christianity to underscore his contention that self-contemplation is
both possible and a mystical dead end. For Zaehner and Buber, the
self can be a delightful trap for the mystic. He may, therefore, settle
for far less than the one true God. He may immerse himself in a form
of narcissistic enstasy and simply lose himself in himself, but "never
meet God." To know oneself or to experience oneself in depth, for
many commentators, is not necessarily to know or to experience the
One who is more intimate to me than myself.

Theistic mysticism is Zaehner's third mystical stage. Loving
union with God is its hallmark. It "represents the return of the spirit
to its immortal ground, which is God" (p. 168). Love mystics know
experientially that God is in them and that they have become one
with God through love. In a powerful chapter entitled, "God Is Love
and God in Love,"[10] Zaehner gives much evidence for this type of
mysticism existing even outside of Christianity.

Although Zaehner tends towards the language of merging to
explain the unity between the mystic and God, he carefully distinguishes union with God from non-theistic, absolute identity with
God. God does not annihilate the individual, for Zaehner, but leaves
her at least enough of the self to experience the blessings of loving
union. The theistic mystic may be thoroughly permeated by the

Divine—like a creaturely sponge in the Divine Ocean—but she never loses her own identity.

One of Zaehner's critics, Ninian Smart, accepts the distinction between nature mysticism and Zaehner's two others as "correct and valuable." On the other hand, Smart prefers to classify nature experiences as "numinous," because the "numinous experience . . . has an outer and thunderous quality not characteristic of the cloud of unknowing within. For this reason it is best to draw a rough distinction between numinous and mystical experience."[11] Zaehner, however, would underscore the seeming identity of inner and outer in nature mystical experiences and mysticism's "essence and keynote" as union. The nature mystic experiences a very deep union with the world to the extent that she actually seems to be the world and the world seems to be she.

Smart rejects, moreover, Zaehner's distinction between monistic and theistic mysticism. He maintains that they are essentially the same, differ only because of the mystic's lifestyle and his interpretation of his experience, and that his truth-claims depend upon factors extrinsic to the mystical experiences themselves. He likewise accuses Zaehner of invalidly imposing Christian theological, philosophical, and moral judgments upon non-Christian traditions to interpret their experiences by way of extrinsic criteria. This, Smart argues, can cut both ways.

On the other hand, Smart would consider Stace's absolute distinction between so-called pure experience and interpretation as somewhat naive, for "experiences are always in some degree interpreted."[12] To defend his thesis that all mysticisms are essentially the same, Smart insists that "there are differing degrees of interpretation."[13] He distinguishes, moreover, between auto- and hetero-interpretation, either with a high or low degree of ramification. Auto-interpretation with a low degree of ramification involves the mystic's own interpretation and is as phenomenologically accurate and theologically neutral as possible; with a high degree of ramification, the mystic's interpretation of his own experiences draws heavily from his theological, dogmatic tradition. Hetero-interpretation with a low degree of ramification involves someone from a different tradition interpreting the mystic's experiences, again as phenomeno-

logically accurate and theologically neutral as possible; with a high
degree of ramification, again drawing heavily from the interpreter's
own theological, dogmatic tradition. For Smart, "it would therefore
seem to be a sound principle to try to seek a low hetero-interpretation coinciding well with a low auto-interpretation."[14]

Zaehner is, therefore, representative of those authors who maintain the Christian mystics' claim to experience differentiated unity
with God. Like Underhill, moreover, he emphasizes both the notion
of unity and the "object" with which the mystic unites. He writes:
"Mysticism is the realization of unity; and unless you have a clear
idea of what that unity is, you are liable to unite with the most
improbable entities" (p. 140).

For Zaehner and others, the mystic's religious tradition, the
techniques he employs, his intentions, his ability to discern "spirits,"
etc., may very well lead him to unite with the God of Love, the Silent
God, the unity of all created things, the depths of the self, or a
variety and hosts of archetypal powers either good or evil. Some of
these unions will bring about varying degrees of peace and fulfillment; others will bring chaos and destruction. The Christian knows,
however, that because only one is holy, the mysticism of mysticisms
is that which leads to full union with the God of Love.

Although Zaehner is known mainly for his vitriolic stance
against Huxley's psychedelic claims, for his severe criticisms of
monistic forms of Hinduism and Islam, and for his exposition of pan-
en-henic, isolation, and theistic mysticisms, his more positive approach to the great religions of the world in his *Concordant Discord:
The Interdependence of the Faiths* has been undeservedly neglected.
This book highlights another very important Zaehner thesis: all
mystics do not speak the same language nor convey the same message, even within one particular religious tradition.

Against those who emphasize the superiority of Western theistic
mysticisms over the religions of the East, Zaehner points out the
profound love-mysticisms of differentiated unity found in some
forms of Hinduism and Buddhism. Taoism's appreciation for the
social obligations for a mystical return to the One attracted him as
well as the Confucian humanistic and radically social mystical dimensions.

Summary

Zaehner stands, therefore, as a powerful counterpoint to the thesis that all mysticisms are essentially one and the same. From the viewpoint of some contemporary Thomistic philosophers, moreover, the human person is essentially spirit-in-world. To be a person means to be fundamentally referred to God, to the unity of all created things, and to self. Within this context, Zaehner's three distinct mystical states make much sense.

He presents a good description of a nature mysticism which may lead to the heights of personal integration or to the depths of madness. With Buber and Raguin, he cautions against a mysticism of isolation and solipsism in which the mystic never gets beyond the self. His defense of theistic mysticism's claim to an experience of differentiated unity is counterpointed by Smart's insistence that interpretation and not experience is at work here.

If one maintains with much of contemporary Catholic theology that God's grace is universally given and always universally at work (even if only secretly, at times), can one speak, as Zaehner does, of a natural mysticism, or a mysticism that is only the absorption with the self, or with the world of nature—stressing a contradistinction from grace, a minimizing sense to "only"—if God's universal salvific will holds? Would it not be better to say that the mystic in question has apparently opted for a center, a treasure, other than the "best" one of the God of Love?

Zaehner's profound treatment of various mystical traditions and his openness to some of the mystical traditions of the East provide a suitable transition point for the next chapters dealing with mysticism as a way of life, the Eastern-turn, and the Eastern-turn criticized.

4
Mysticism as a Way of Life I

Evelyn Underhill

Many contemporary commentators unhesitatingly endorse Evelyn Underhill's *Mysticism* as the best one-volume study of mysticism.[1] Friedrich Schlegel once wrote: "A classic is a writing that is never fully understood. But those that are educated and educate themselves must always want to learn more from it."[2] It is in this sense that Underhill's book is a classic. She has grounded a tradition in which mystical scholarship is researched, studied, and interpreted. Her strong emphasis upon mysticism as a way of life involving various stages, moreover, sharply sets her off from many authors considered above.[3]

Even a brief glance at the structure of Underhill's book reveals a profound grasp of the nature of mysticism by its intelligent distinction between "the Mystic Fact" and "the Mystic Way." Under the former she discusses the characteristics of mysticism and its relationship to vitalism, psychology, philosophy, theology, symbolism, and magic. Under the latter, she emphasizes that mysticism is a complete way of life, not transient experiences or occasional visions. Hence, she explains mysticism as an authentic life process, involving transitory experiences, but transcending them with an ordered movement toward perfect consummation with the God of Love.

Mysticism discloses the deep desire of the human person to surrender to the Mystery of total love. In the great mystics, moreover, this desire dominates both their entire lives and consciousness.

Although a surrender to this tendency transforms the mystic's personality, promotes growth, and brings about extraordinary experiences, Underhill does not consider this enough. In strong counterpoint to many commentators who focus sharply on the above, she emphasizes the living, unchanging God who initiates, motivates, and directs the mystic's quest. In short, mysticism is not primarily concerned with altered states of consciousness, peak experiences, various "highs," or even with self-actualization. The God of Love gives this way of life its proper sanction.

Underhill disagrees with James' four marks of the mystical consciousness and gives five of her own. First of all, mysticism is active, practical, involves the entire person, and brings forth experience in its most intense form. Rather than being passive and theoretical, genuine mysticism is human life in its most difficult and authentic form. It blends surrender, love, and spiritual insight.

Secondly, it aims only for what is spiritual and not of this world. The mystic's experience of God annihilates all desire for knowledge, happiness, virtue, or occult power. To be sure, frequently these accompany the mystical quest. Yet, the genuine mystic wants only God, and this deepest desire reorganizes, destroys, or transforms all lesser cravings.

Third, only Love explains mysticism. Repudiating every other transcendental theory and practice, the mystic remains essentially a lover. The genuine mystic is not merely interested in "Reality." He is not busy with exploring reality in the way a scientist would. The mystic is in love with a Reality which is both living and personal. The God of Love has created a homeward-turning love within every person. When this love dominates the person's entire being and consciousness, it distinguishes the authentic mystic from the philosopher, artist, magician, etc., although these may receive their initial spark from mysticism.

Fourth, a qualitatively transformed life comes about through union with the living God. Mysticism bestows both an experience of the Real and the mystic's transformation. The experience of Holiness itself demands and brings forth conversion, the felt-need to be like what was experienced. The God-experience demands holiness, sanctity, and the remaking of the self on a higher level. For Underhill, the mystic is the religious genius who possesses the requisite psychological make-up, moral tenacity, and heroic concentration required for this "inward alchemy," the transformation of the old man into the new.

Lastly, "true Mysticism is never self-seeking" (p. 92). Once again, Underhill emphasizes that the mystic transforms her being, because she willingly renounced all claims to happiness. The genuine mystic proves the Gospel saying that only those who lose their lives gain them.

No author thus far has so accurately captured and described the phases and stages of mystical life as Underhill. She calls the first stage "the awakening of the Self to consciousness of Divine Reality" (p. 169). Be it abruptly or gradually, something happens to shift the person's center of gravity, to disrupt his basic personal equilibrium, to transform his affective, intellectual, and moral stance. Tides of consolation and desolation, oscillations between periods of unrest, stress, etc., and great feelings of joy and exaltation accompany this conversion. The inner and outer world look and feel differently. The discrepancy between perfect Love and the imperfect world or between what he is and should be may suddenly open the person's eyes.

The second stage involves "the purification of the Self" (pp. 198f.). The double vision of God and the self highlights the contrast between God's holiness, beauty, purity, and Reality, and the self's sinfulness, vileness, and manifold illusions. The mystic painfully experiences the incredible distance which separates her from her heart's desire. Moreover, she becomes haunted by feelings of contrition, unworthiness, and the need for penance. But she realizes that purgation is no less a privilege than illumination.

The elimination of some of the obstacles to the mystic's quest occurs only through self-simplification, cleansing, stripping, mortification, and discipline. The self instinctively knows that it must regain control of its lower vital centers and the surface intellect to begin to detach itself successfully from everything other than the Divine Reality. At this stage, the self seems to target self-love and the manifold vanities of its surface consciousness as its main enemies. It is willing to undertake pain and suffering to break out of the prison of its narrow individuality to unite with greater Life.

Having been purified from sensuality, having obtained many strengthening virtues, the purged and intensified consciousness reaches the contemplative stage par excellence, "the illumination of the Self" (pp. 232f.). Illuminated by Reality itself, the mystic now enjoys "the first mystic life," a multi-leveled stage and life beyond which most mystics never progress. To some extent, he shares this life with the great artists, prophets, seers, and philosophers. But, he has, in fact, parted company with them.

Three types of experience, moreover, usually accompany mystical illumination. The first bestows a deep and joyful sense of the presence of God. Underhill calls it a "pleasure state of the intensest kind" (p. 241). The purified self, however, awesomely contemplates the Absolute, experiences a joyful relationship in which the dichotomy between his self and the Absolute remains. Although he experiences a certain fellowship with the Absolute, it is not the consummation of love, at once both intimate and adorable. He is "betrothed," but not yet married. He tastes a deep and satisfying harmony with God, but not yet a total self-surrender and self-loss in the God of Love. As Underhill says: "The real distinction between the Illuminative and the Unitive Life is that in Illumination the individuality of the subject—however profound his spiritual consciousness, however close his apparent communion with the infinite—remains separate and intact" (p. 246).

The second type of experience given during illumination revolves around "a deep intuitional knowledge of the 'secret plan' " (p. 233). The mystic begins to see the world from the viewpoint of the Absolute. Underhill calls this a sacramental expansion, and not an ascetic concentration, of consciousness. As she says, "the discovery of the Perfect One self-revealed in the Many, not the forsaking of the Many in order to find the One" (p. 254), characterizes this experience. The mystic tastes from the heart both God's transcendence and immanence, and experiences the harmony which exists in all the various manifestations of life.

Through her progressive appropriation of more and more transcendental life, the mystic begins to experience now her radically deepened and enhanced self. With a consciousness intensified both in the direction of God and the world, she may find this depth consciousness expressing itself in locutions, auditions, automatic writing, etc. She is not perfect at this stage, but the tradition does call her "proficient."

As the mystic ascends the mystical ladder, he usually receives visions, locutions, and a great variety of other secondary mystical phenomena. While some of these phenomena may result from hallucination, projection, wish-fulfillment, or a general pathological condition, others cannot be so readily dismissed. Genuine mystical phenomena possess a life-enhancing quality, are "sources of helpful energy, charity, and courage" (p. 270), and "are the media by which the 'seeing self' truly approaches the Absolute" (p. 270).

They frequently occur at critical moments in the mystic's life to bestow love, wisdom, goodness, calmness, strength, and authority. On the other hand, in the life of any mystic they are usually a mixed phenomenon because they reflect both the mystic's increasing wholeness and his decreasing brokenness. For Underhill, visions and locutions artistically express for the mystic what music, poetry, and paintings express for the artist. They exteriorize, therefore, the mystic's inner life, allowing it to penetrate all levels of consciousness in creative ways.

Underhill, however, has not overlooked the varying quality and depth of these mystical phenomena. The mystic may perceive with his corporeal senses, his "imaginative senses," or his "spiritual senses." The mystic, then, may see, hear, taste, smell, or touch with his physical, interior, and spiritual faculties things normally imperceptible; he will also value and trust these perceptions, the more interior the depth at which they have been perceived.

Genuine mysticism proceeds according to the laws of organic development. It is a life-process which also develops the mystic's personality. Although alone on her mystical quest, she must submit to discipline, be educated, and pay careful attention to experience, tradition, and the mystical society in particular. Being aware of the Absolute, to contemplate it and eventually unite with it, she must gradually develop her ability to concentrate.

Contemplation is the way the mystic pulls away from the external world for total concentration of the personality. In order to awaken the deeper self and to initiate the birth of the new self, profound self-forgetting attentiveness is required. For Underhill, "introversion" plays the key role in the mystical life.

At the earliest stages, introversion demands deliberate, difficult spiritual gymnastics. During the purgative stage, the mystic becomes meditative or recollected. Breaking with the obvious, the self willfully turns toward the inward path. The first degree of love demands a quieting of the surface consciousness, a "one-ing" of oneself around the object of one's desire.

At the illuminative stage, this introversion is the prayer of simplicity or quiet. Much greater inwardness, passivity, interior silence, calmness of the surface consciousness, and the deep sense that "something" is there characterize this stage. The mystic experiences the paradox of deprivation, yet having; emptiness, yet completion. Free self-giving and self-emptying are now possible. For Underhill, "it marks the transition from 'natural' to 'supernatural' prayer" (p. 319).

Contemplation, however, is the deepest form of mystical introversion. It involves various degrees and kinds of mystical prayer, from uncontrollable ecstatic flights to God to the more controllable ecstatic, or sinking into the core of one's being, meetings of the mystic with his Beloved. Contemplation is characterized by: "(A) The Totality and Givenness of the Object. (B) Self-Mergence of the Subject" (p. 332). In short, the mystic experiences having received a gift, an attainment not due to his efforts. God reveals Himself, and not some aspect, symbol, or token of His Presence. The mystic now knows God by way of participation in His life, and no longer as a meditative observer. Contemplation contains the paradoxical blending of beatifying vision, communion, intimacy, and emptiness, desert, remoteness, and darkness. True contemplation indicates at least a semi-permanent union with God. For Underhill, these characteristics distinguish contemplation from other forms of mystical introversion.

Contemplation may center upon either God's transcendence or His immanence. In the former, the mystic contemplates God as the "Wholly Other," the "Divine Darkness," or the "Unconditioned One." The ontological difference between God and all created things stands out. The mystic's sense of ignorance, awe, unworthiness, littleness, and self-abasement predominates. God seems strange and unattainable, and the mystic describes Him according to the negative categories of the apophatic tradition, the tradition which stresses that God cannot in any way be comprehended by the mind, only by the heart.[4]

For those who contemplate God's immanence, God is radically Person, Friend, Lover, Bridegroom. The mystic's sense of nearness, love, sweetness, and intimacy predominates. These mystics establish the kataphatic tradition, a tradition which defines God in positive terms. To be sure, one and the same mystic may blend elements from both traditions. Because Christianity believes in an all-transcendent God who became incarnate, a God who is the metaphysical Reality, yet radically personal, hence the Divine Darkness and the Bridegroom, mystical experience must be both negative and affirmative, impersonal and personal.[5]

Contemplation, or the prayer of union with God, reaches a new and higher level when the mystic is subjected to "Ecstasy and Rapture" (pp. 358f.). During normal contemplation, Underhill notes, the mystic freely chooses to ignore the outside world. During ecstasy, however, the mystic "*cannot* attend to it" (p. 358). Ecstasy results from an unusually powerful concentration upon God, and one which produces an "exceptionally favorable state" (p. 358).

Underhill considers ecstasy as "really the name of the outward condition rather than of any one kind of inward experience" (p. 375). The psychophysical conditions which attend contemplation's perfect unity of consciousness, the exclusion of all conceptual thoughts and discursive acts, a love so intense that self-consciousness is lost, a seeming merger with God for a short period of time, is called ecstasy. Still more pointedly, "the true note of ecstasy, however, its only valid distinction from infused contemplation, lies in *entrancement*" (pp. 367–68). Ecstasy seems to be *irresistible* contemplation. She does not, however, identify mysticism and ecstasy.[6]

Many false notions and errors in mystical studies, as Underhill notes, occur from a failure to distinguish between the physical, psychological, and mystical aspects of ecstasy. Some of the physical aspects of ecstasy are: trance, diminished breathing and circulation, coldness and rigidity of body, and a short period of lucidity usually followed by a longer period of complete unconsciousness. Genuine mystical ecstasy produces great inward graces and has after-effects beneficial to both mind and body. The life-enhancing quality of genuine mystical ecstasy distinguishes it from pathological and pseudo-mystical ecstasies.

From the psychological point of view, ecstasy is total mono-ideism. The mystic deliberately pays attention to one thing, and the ecstasy's worth depends upon the value of that one thing. Pure perception and the unification of consciousness also occur.

From the mystical point of view, ecstasy is an especially valued act of perception, for it redirects consciousness toward pure Being. The act of pure apprehension suspends all references to self. It moves toward developing and completing the prayer of union.

Raptures, for Underhill, are abrupt, spontaneous, and violent forms of ecstasies. These frenzied expressions of genius may even do permanent damage. The beneficial effects of raptures predominate, however. Still, they highlight the disharmony which exists between the mystic's transcendental desires and her psychophysical make-up.

Between what Underhill calls "the first mystic life," or the illuminative way, and "the second mystic life," or the unitive way, there is a phase traditionally known as the dark night of the spirit. Mystically speaking, for Underhill, the dark night of the soul is simply the stage which occurs between the illuminative and the unitive stages. Psychologically speaking, it results from exhaustion and expresses a transition stage. The intense strain put upon the mystic from her pursuit of deeper, richer life finally catches up with her. But to attain this deeper, richer life, she has now come to the point where her old unity must be shattered for the total transformation into the new woman.

Underhill lists five characteristics of the dark night of the soul. First of all, the mystic is certain that God has justifiably abandoned her. Second, her sense of sin is far greater than anything she experienced during the purgative way. Third, she comes very close to despair because of emotional boredom, aridity, and spiritual ennui. Fourth, the intellect and will seem powerless. She is astonished at the power of temptation in her life. Finally, she desires to see God as He is, experiences an incredible loneliness because of the Divine Absence, and realizes how trite were her earlier experiences of God.

Underhill is in essential agreement with Maritain when she looks upon the dark night of the soul as what separates the great mystics from "nature" mystics, or the mystical poets, who are mystically illuminated to some degree. During the dark night of the soul, on the other hand, the genuine seekers of God must die mystically. During this period of utter impotence, radical loneliness, complete isolation, chaos, stagnation, unwanted trials and tribulations, the person learns the difficult lesson of selflessness. For love's sake, he bears the burden of lovelessness. This phase aims at the total and final purification of the mystic which destroys the root of self-love. This radical purgation cannot be effected by the mystic. It is the negative side of God's supreme gift of Himself. The mystic's only activity during this period involves an ever-deeper surrender to God's cleansing influx.

The last stage of the mystical life Underhill calls "the Unitive Life" (pp. 413f.). The authentic mystic will settle for nothing less than total union with God. This radical union with God brings about the mystic's "deification," his transformation into God by participation. Spiritually married to God, he is now conscious of sharing the very life, power, and strength of God Himself. This stage bestows authority, conviction, serenity, freedom, and joy. So well integrated is the mystic into God's life, that ecstasies and raptures cease. Two (the mystic and God) have become one, and yet remain two.

Spiritual marriage, however, results in a divine, spiritual fecundity, a point frequently overlooked by writers on mysticism. For Underhill, "This reproductive power is one of the greatest marks of the theopathetic life" (p. 432). Utterly aware of his divine sonship, the mystic wants to communicate what he has received. Plunged into God's life, this love comes to fruition in the world's "great actives." Underhill stresses the practical side of those united with transcendental life. They are frequently the great poets, artists, religious and social reformers, national heroes, etc. Lost in transcendental life, they return "to fertilize those levels of existence from which it sprang" (p. 414). Although they take their responsibility most seriously for being fertile, spiritual parents, their joy, gaiety, playfulness, and "spirit of dalliance" mark them.

In what is perhaps too sweeping a criticism of Eastern mysticisms, Underhill notes that they demand another stage beyond union. Total self-annihilation, perfect loss of all individuality through merging with the Infinite, and no return to the world characterize this stage.[7] As she writes: "In the mystics of the West, the highest forms of Divine Union impel the self to some sort of active, rather than passive life: and this is now recognized by the best authorities as the true distinction beteen Christian and non-Christian mysticism" (p. 172).

Because all of us have in germ what fully blossoms in the lives of the great mystics, the study of mysticism, for Underhill, is extremely important. "The adventure of the great mystics . . . is a master-key to man's puzzle," she writes. "The mystics, expert mountaineers, go before him; and show him, if he cares to learn, the way to freedom, to reality, to peace" (p. 448). These spiritual giants are our brothers and sisters who show us what authentic human living is and offer us paradigms for our own spiritual growth. Their achievements belong not only to themselves, but to all. In short, we can follow the low road of the mystics' high road.

Summary

By delineating mysticism as a way of life which focuses exclusively on loving God and seeking union with Him, Underhill clearly distinguishes herself from commentators who emphasize mysticism as a series of unrelated psychological peak experiences, or as altered states of consciousness. The mystic's love motivation and successful passage through the dark night of the soul, moreover, set the mystic apart from those seeking occult power, from nature mystics, poets, seers, and philosophers.

Her careful exposition of the mystic's conversion to, purification by, illumination by, and eventual union with the God of love merits special attention. Visions, locutions, and other secondary mystical phenomena, moreover, are discussed within the context of mysticism as a way of life. Valuable, too, is her explanation of the dark night of the soul as a God-induced, mystical death of the old self for the self's total transformation. Unlike many commentators, moreover, she underscores the "spiritual fecundity," or pragmatic and social concerns, which flows from total union with God. Although she defends union with differentiation, not self-annihilation or merging with God, as the mystic's goal, she insists upon both the personal and the impersonal quality of that union.

Her description of contemplation as "introversion," the mystic's "medium," the semi-permanent union with God, which is paradoxically experienced in a darkness which is light, is excellent. She also explains ecstasy as irresistible contemplation and rapture as sudden and violent contemplation. Unlike many commentators, however, she does not equate mysticism with ecstasy and rapture.

Underhill can be listed with those commentators who see mysticism as essentially the same the world over. She also emphasizes that the mystics are paradigms of authentic human life, a point made by many commentators. Some would fault Underhill, however, for her lack of appreciation of the Eastern mystical tradition, for her tendency to treat mysticism almost exclusively from a Christian viewpoint, and for her failure to underscore the workings of God's grace even in non-Christian mysticisms. It should be remembered, however, how far ahead of the scholarship of her day Underhill was, how easy it is to criticize her in the light of contemporary scholarship still not widely accepted, and how much of her work still remains valid.

5
Mysticism as a Way of Life II

Thomas Merton

Some commentators have pointed out that Thomas Merton contributed very little of originality to the study of mysticism. Others would agree, however, with Raymond Bailey "that his greatest contribution was the particularity of his person and the synthesizing and contemporizing of ancient and universal truths."[1] One clearly sees in Merton's life the lived paradoxes, the partial syntheses, the tensions, the joys, and the agonies of one whose primary concern was mystical union with God in an age of Auschwitz, Hiroshima, Vietnam, the Watts riot, Harlem, civil rights, and Aquarius. Many find in Merton the prototype of those for whom mysticism must be a way of life involving progressive growth in union with God, with other persons, and with creation in general. Finally, his life illustrates the impossibility of separating mysticism from the intellectual, institutional, social, and traditional factors out of which it arises.

For Merton, because of Adam's fall, the human person is exiled from God and from his true self to live in a world of illusion. The person must, therefore, reorient his entire life and being around God to achieve union with God in Christ. To become a new person in Christ requires mystical transformation, re-creation, and restoration of the human as created in the image of the God of love. As Merton says: "The battle is with 'man' and yet it is with God, for it is the battle of our exterior self with the interior self, the 'agent' which is

51

the likeness of God in our soul and which appears at the first sight to be utterly opposed to the only self we know."[2]

Merton speaks of a twofold mystical movement of death and rebirth. The genuine contemplative descends into his own nothingness, helplessness, frustrations, infidelities, ignorance, and confusion to experience his total need for God. Through this mystical death, the contemplative is liberated, purified, and enlightened in perfect love. This mystical descent into one's own hell results in an experience of love-wisdom so powerful that it overcomes all other loves and desires. Contemplative prayer, for Merton, is "simply the preference for the desert, for emptiness, for poverty. . . . "[3]

The themes of inner poverty, solitude, emptiness, nakedness, etc., recur constantly in Merton's writings. We should "let ourselves be brought naked and defenceless into the center of that dread where we stand alone before God in our nothingness."[4] Because the self is not its own center, but is centered on God, the contemplative must pass through his own soul, transcend himself, and finally lose himself in the solitude and mystery of God working within. For Merton, however, "it is dread and dread alone, that drives a man out of this private sanctuary in which his solitude becomes horrible to himself without God."[5]

Mystical prayer is essentially a prayer of the heart. The deepest psychological foundations of one's personality wherein self-awareness transcends analytical reflection open out and reach for their true identity in God. Merton's outlook, however, is one of crisis. God is known especially in stripping. "To receive the word of the Cross means the acceptance of a complete self-emptying, a *kenosis,* in union with the self-emptying of Christ 'obedient unto death.' "[6] The deepening of serious faith and progress in mystical prayer require the experience of dying to self, of self-emptiness, and utter nakedness. Merton subscribes to the mystical paradox that one recovers one's true identity in God only when one no longer has a self.[7]

True contemplation, therefore, can never be merely technique, methods, or a system. It is primarily a personal vocation, a free gift from God, and a mystery of divine love. It fosters an attitude and outlook of faith, openness, reverence, attention, trust, supplication, expectation, joy, and true emptiness. "It is the contemplative, silent, 'empty' and apparently useless element in the life of prayer," writes

Merton, "which makes it truly a *life*."[8] For this reason, although Merton emphasizes the value of prayer for individual, social, and worldly transformation, he has harsh words for those who exploit prayer for the purposes of "pseudo-activism." Genuine prayer expresses the person's *entire* individual, social, and worldly life in its relationship to God.

Merton locates mysticism's essence in an experience of differentiated unity, a union in which God and the contemplative become one, yet remain two. "I want to make it quite clear," he writes, "that the whole essence of contemplative prayer is that the division between subject and object disappears."[9] The contemplative dynamic of kenotic transformation in which the person empties and transcends himself concludes in an experience of God as Subject. During this supraconscious experience, the person becomes aware of the difference between her daily self and her "transcendent Self." This transcendent Self "is metaphysically distinct from the Self of God and yet perfectly identified with that Self by love and freedom, so that there appears to be but one Self."[10] Merton further describes a love mysticism of differentiated unity in theological terms strongly reminiscent of the *Cloud of Unknowing* and St. John of the Cross. He writes:

> However, the union between the soul and God in love is close and so complete that the only remaining distinction between them is the fundamental distinction between the two separate substances ... the only trace of distinction that remains between them is the fact that what is God's by nature is the soul's by participation and by God's free gift, that is by love.[11]

A certain simplicity permeates Merton's mystical theology. He wants us to experience, to grasp, and to accept God's personal love for us in Christ so that we can be ourselves. The theme of being oneself frequently appears in his writings. But the divine image which we are manifests itself only through our union with Christ. Merton's mysticism is anthropocentric, i.e., focuses upon human transformation and becoming the "New Man," because he fully takes into account the meaning of the Incarnation. The person of

Jesus Christ plays a key role even in Merton's preference for the dark, silent contemplation of unknowing and forgetting in the apophatic tradition, a tradition solidly rooted in Christ's self-emptying. Because of Christ's *kenosis,* Merton defines contemplation as "a deep participation in the Christ-life, a spiritual sharing in the union of God and man which is the hypostatic union."[12] One reaches full union with God only by way of self-emptying. The paradox is that everything human in Christ is thereby divine, and for that reason more richly and deeply human.

Merton emphatically criticized contemporary attempts to reduce mystical experience to regression, aesthetics, self-conscious awareness, or even moral transcendence. Although he praised the transformative value of contemplation for the individual and for society, he insisted that

> What really matters in spiritual experience is not its interiority, or its natural purity, or the joy, light, exaltation, and transforming effect it may seem to have: these things are secondary and accidental. What matters is not what one feels, but *what really takes place* beyond the level of feeling or experience. In genuine contemplation, what takes place is a contact between the inmost reality of the created person and the infinite Reality of God.[13]

Like Underhill, therefore, Merton will settle for nothing less than the Christian God of Love who is the origin, dynamism, and goal of the mystical quest.

Merton directed some of his harshest words toward the bogus interiority and pseudo-mysticism of quietism. For an age prone to value all inner experiences as the same and to value so highly techniques for mystical introversion and enstasy, Merton writes:

> Nor can a person become a contemplative merely by "blacking out" sensible realities and remaining alone with himself in darkness . . . enter[ing] into an artificial darkness of his own making. He is not alone with God, but alone with himself . . . an idol: his own complacent identity . . . lost in himself, in a state of inert, primitive and infantile

narcissism. . . . It is purely the nothingness of a finite being
left to himself and absorbed in his own triviality.[14]

Even in mysticism, therefore, nothing sometimes is really nothing. The absence of knowledge need not necessarily be accompanied
by the presence of wisdom, the hallmark of genuine mysticism. A
self-induced solitude may, in fact, turn out to be isolation, a nothingness which does not have the all of St. John of the Cross. It is simply
spiritual pride, the most subtle and deadliest enemy of genuine
contemplation, "the love of one's spiritualized, purified, and 'empty'
self."[15] This type of self-emptying leaves the pseudo-contemplative
full of self, complacent, with no real concern for God, for others, or
the world. This primitive and infantile narcissism "may confirm us
in delusions and harden us against the fundamental awareness of our
real condition."[16] This spiritual vacuum, blank, devoid of genuine
mystical love and wisdom, indicates for Merton that

> to become a Yogi and to be able to commit moral and
> intellectual suicide whenever you please, without the neces-
> sity of actually dying, to be able to black out your mind by
> the incantation of half-articulate charms and to enter into a
> state of annihilation, in which all the faculties are inactive
> and the soul is inert, as it were dead—all this may well
> appeal to certain minds as a refined and rather pleasant
> way to getting even with the world and with society, and
> with God Himself for that matter.[17]

Pseudo-mysticism intersects with another important theme for
Merton: illusion. Sin has wounded the human person at the very
roots of her being. The person thereby exists in a state of guilty
estrangement from God, from others, and from her true self. Still,
the refusal to acknowledge this radical brokenness perdures, for the
human person not only refuses but is also incapable of facing this
inner truth without God's grace. Pseudo-mysticism is especially
pernicious, because it simply reinforces the perverse attachment we
have to a self which is essentially illusory. Modern society, social life,
and we, all conspire to fabricate a false self which lives an essential
lie. If lies and fabrication harm even the daily relationships between

persons, the lie which falsifies the relationship between the person and the ground of her being is a disaster. Genuine prayer fosters the experience of dread which forces the person to face the nothingness and helplessness of the human situation. Dread is, moreover,

> an awareness of infidelity as unrepented and without grace as *unrepentable*. It is the deep, confused, metaphysical awareness of a *basic antagonism between the self and God* due to estrangement from him by perverse attachment to a "self" which is mysterious and illusory.[18]

Not a few have found Merton's transposition of the somewhat legalistic, extrinsicistic emphases of the traditional view on sin into the categories of existentialist philosophy most helpful.

Merton highly valued the transformative and life-giving qualities of the monastic tradition and life. He knew that initiation into a traditional religious way with its implicit and explicit checks and balances could provide the only genuine foundation for mystical ascent. The authentic mystic needs the wisdom of experienced persons and the support of a community which itself has experienced and fostered genuine mystical consciousness. Even Merton's sporadic, but strong, attractions to the eremitical life (which he never reconciled with his even stronger attractions for community and deep friendships) were partially nurtured by the traditional writings of those who had led and fostered the hermit life before him.

One finds in Merton a creative rediscovery, retrieval, and transposition of the monastic tradition. Monastic life in all its traditional aspects, but interlaced wtih a deep reading of the desert fathers, the classical Christian mystics, contemporary existential philosophy, Freud, Jung, Maritain, Gilson, Teilhard de Chardin, Huxley, William Blake, the Russian mystics, Quakerism, Taoism, Buddhism, and an empathy for contemporary social issues, nurtured in Merton "a way of resting in him whom we have *found,* who loves us, who is near to us, who comes to us to draw us to himself."[19] Community life, the hardships of common life, psalmody, liturgy, the sacraments, physical labor, asceticism, Scripture, the study of theology and contemporary thought, moral discipline, solitary contemplation patterned after Christ's solitary prayer at night—all of these centered on the purity of heart necessary for the monk's unconditional and total surrender to the God of love. But he likewise insisted that certain ascetic and monastic practices could become an actual barrier to progress, if clung to as ends in themselves.

Merton dubbed the so-called opposition between liturgical and private prayer, between official public prayer and spontaneous personal prayer a "modern fiction." Although deeply attracted to the silent, dark apophatic way of St. John of the Cross, he possessed a profound theology of the kataphatic way, the way of affirmation. He wrote:

> The function of image, symbol, poetry, music, chant, and of ritual . . . is to open up the inner self of the contemplative, to incorporate the senses and the body in the totality of the self-orientation to God that is necessary for worship and meditation.[20]

Apophatic prayer needs a kataphatic matrix in which to mature. For Merton, his "thorough and mature 'monastic culture' "[21] fostered the higher levels of prayer.

Merton favored the monastic "desert" atmosphere which seriously challenged contemporary secular values. He spoke loudly against the dehumanizing of the person through the idolatry of consumption, technology, science, machinery, power, and activism. He preferred agrarian values and a life close to nature in which everything worked harmoniously to obey God's will, a view shared by some writers.[22]

Merton deeply loved the monastic life and the desert, but he also loved all of life, others, and the world. He insisted that mystical prayer penetrate every aspect and dimension of Christian existence. Like Francis de Sales' "ecstasy of work and life," Merton pointed out that mystical prayer must remain firmly rooted in daily life. It must foster "a simple respect for the concrete realities of everyday life, for nature, for the body, for one's work, one's friends, one's surroundings, etc."[23] The mystical life does not blind the monk to the world, but transforms his vision of it.

The genuine contemplative takes full responsibility for himself, for others, and for the world. He finds his identity not only in God, but also in others. The contemplative life is impossible without a genuine love for others. Merton saw contemplation, moreover, as releasing energies which could transform the world through deeply social action. The monk's chief service to the world, for Merton, consisted in "this silence, this listening, this questioning, this humble and courageous exposure to what the world ignores about itself—both good and evil."[24] Because Merton had confronted his own humanity and the world's at its core, he could speak convincingly and accurately about the sicknesses of contemporary life. And for him, the "contemplative will ... concern himself with the same problems as other people, but he will try to get to the spiritual and metaphysical roots of these problems, not by analysis but by simplicity."[25]

Merton criticized the narcissistic quietism, the substituting of drugs for love, and the sickly preoccupation with self which characterize some of contemporary life. But he likewise condemned the pseudo-spirituality of activism. He realized that no amount of social action could replace spiritual transformation and enlightenment. He had clearly perceived the dangers of political delusions, of trusting in slogans and the tactics of various pressure groups. He even questioned whether or not his own need for "helping others" and for "being open" had not led him into real illusion. As he says,

> He who attempts to act and do things for others or for the world without deepening his own self-understanding, freedom, integrity and capacity to love, will not have anything to give others. He will communicate to them nothing but the contagion of his own obsessions, his aggressiveness, his ego-centered ambitions, his delusions about ends and means, his doctrinaire prejudices and ideas.[26]

Genuine prayer, for Merton, held the key to enlightened and truly transformative social action.

Because everyone is born with the desire to know the Truth, the mystical life can be found in everyone, at least anonymously. Christian baptism, moreover, deepens this universal potentiality for mystical experience. Merton emphasized that real mystics, i.e., those who have received explicitly infused mystical prayer, will always be somewhat few and rare. Manifest mystical prayer requires a special vocation. On the other hand, Merton held that the mystical life is the normal way of Christian perfection. Every Christian life contains at least a dormant and hidden aspect of infused prayer and a call to "masked" or "hidden contemplation."

"Hidden" or "masked contemplation" occurs when people experience the meaninglessness, emptiness, and uselessness of their lives, but persevere in silent trust and hope. Ordinary life lived without fuss and fanfare, but in courage and naked faith, can also be masked contemplation. The hidden or masked contemplatives, moreover, may devote themselves unselfishly to secular life and the service of others. As Merton says:

> There are many Christians who serve God with great purity of soul and perfect self-sacrifice in the active life. Their vocation does not allow them to find the solitude and silence and leisure in which to empty their minds entirely of created things and to lose themselves in God alone. They are too busy serving Him in His children on earth. At the same time, their minds and temperaments do not fit them for a purely contemplative life; they would know no peace without exterior activity. Although they are active laborers they are also *hidden contemplatives* because of the great purity of heart maintained in them by obedience, fraternal charity, self-sacrifice and perfect abandonment to God's Will in all that they do and suffer. . . . They enjoy a kind of "masked" contemplation.[27]

This quote illustrates that Merton refused to reduce mysticism to a gnostic interiority reserved for a spiritual elite. In fact, the very hiddenness of this type of contemplation has special advantages. "Since contemplation is communion with a hidden God in His own hiddenness," Merton writes, "it tends to be pure in proportion as it is itself hidden."[28]

Merton was convinced that a profound desire for inner unity and direct communion with the Absolute existed everywhere in the world. Certain individuals and communities in the world's great religions attempt to live out the full implications and consequences of their beliefs. Merton saw in contemporary Christianity, however, activist, secular, and anti-mystical tendencies which conceded far too much to Marxist assumptions about religion being the opium of the people. He had found, moreover, in the contemplative traditions of the East a certain outlook on which our spiritual and even our physical survival may depend. He was also quick to acknowledge the natural affinity of Eastern and Western mysticisms on a number of significant issues. During his trip to Asia, he wrote:

> I come as a pilgrim who is anxious to obtain not just information, not just "facts" about other monastic traditions, but to drink from ancient sources of monastic vision and experience. I seek not only to learn more (quantitatively) about religion and about monastic life, but to become a better and more enlightened monk (qualitatively) myself.[29]

Summary

Merton blended in his person traditional monastic and contemporary Christian values. His person and writings highlight, moreover, the requisite transposition of the traditional mystical life into its contemporary setting. He emphasized mysticism as a way of life in which the person faces his own inner emptiness, destroys the illusion of self-worship, and reorients his entire life to God, others, and the world. Mysticism, moreover, is not a technique but a vocation by which a person becomes a "new man" in Christ, a "transcendent Self," living in differentiated unity with the God of Love. Like Zaehner, he castigated the tendency of some mysticisms toward "infantile narcissism."

He prophetically criticized both contemporary secular values which demean the human person and the pseudo-activism of some contemporary Christians who devalue the contemplative tradition. Blending the best of the apophatic and kataphatic mystical traditions, Merton saw the monk as a social force because he faced himself in radical truth. He also held for a "masked contemplation" which manifests itself in an active life of self-sacrifice for others. His appreciation of the mystical traditions of the East, moreover, provides a good transition point for the next section.

6
Christianity's Eastern Turn

Thomas Merton: Looking East

In the spirit of Vatican II's creative openness to the great religions of the East, Merton pleaded for a genuine dialogue with them. He was firmly convinced that Christianity had much to learn from Eastern religion. He challenged the anti-mystical views of "the new consciousness"[1] which sprang both from Barthian neo-Orthodoxy's biblical renewal and progressive Catholic activists' Marxist emphases. Far from being life-denying, selfish navel-gazing, drug-induced trance, and moral and intellectual suicide, Eastern religions frequently promote a quiet sense of personhood, a sense of the human, a taste for cosmic unity, peace, and an affirmation of life. He discovered in the Eastern traditions, moreover, an unusually effective way of smashing the illusionary world of Western and Marxist materialism. Speculating that the great religious leaders of Hinduism, Buddhism, Islam, etc., were mystics in the supernatural sense, he found in all the world's great monastic traditions "a special concern with inner transformation, a deepening of consciousness toward an eventual breakthrough and discovery of a transcendent dimension of life beyond that of the ordinary empirical self and of ethical and pious observances."[2]

Both Zen and Tibetan mysticism held special attraction for Merton. Zen's severe, simple style of direction is especially good at destroying pious illusions and spiritual self-importance, unmasking self-righteousness, and exploding one's false self in the interests of the true self. Both Christians and Buddhists, according to Merton, could practice Zen, "if by Zen we mean precisely the quest for direct and pure experience on a metaphysical level, liberated from verbal formulas and linguistic preconceptions."[3] Because Zen is concrete, direct, non-doctrinal, and existential, and comes to grips with life, it has much to offer Christianity. Merton agreed with the Dalai Lama that "one could not attain anything in the spiritual life without total dedication, continued effort, experienced guidance, real discipline, and the combination of wisdom and method (which is stressed by Tibetan mysticism)."[4] That Merton had once cryptically remarked that he had decided "to become as good a Buddhist as I can"[5] should, perhaps, be understood in the above context.

Merton discovered in Zen an exceptional way of being attentive to and aware of reality with a trans-conceptual, trans-emotional, transformed consciousness. The Zen adept penetrates the natural, metaphysical ground of being and attains "realization," or enlightenment. Zen attempts "to get back, as far as possible, to the pure unarticulated and unexplained ground of direct experience."[6] During a supra-conscious and metaphysical awakening, a pure consciousness of wisdom-intuition, in which the difference between subject and object disappears, emerges from what Merton calls the "transcendental unconsciousness." The perfect awareness of pure presence results when the isolated ego-self stops dominating the center of consciousness and the transcendental unconscious takes over. The transcendental unconscious is the person's true self which is one with all of creation. Zen enlightenment, for Merton, seems to be

> a kind of natural ecstasy in which our own being recognizes in itself a transcendental kinship with every other being that exists and, as it were, flows out of itself to possess all being and returns to itself to find all being in itself.[7]

This is consciousness of Being, and not a "consciousness of" anything. "The metaphysical intuition of Being is an intuition of a ground of openness"[8] which is begotten through self-giving, love, letting-go, and ecstasy. The self thereby discovers that its real center is not the tiny island of the empirical ego, but reality itself.

Christianity and Buddhism, for Merton, really do not contradict each other. Comparing Christianity and Zen Buddhism, moreover, is like comparing math and tennis. Christianity offers a living experience of union in Christ; Zen, an immediate awareness of the unity of the visible and invisible creation. Christianity is a religion of grace and divine gift and is based upon supernatural revelation. "Zen is then," for Merton, "not Kerygma but realization, not revelation but consciousness, not news from the Father who sends His Son into this world, but awareness of the ontological ground of our own being here and now, right in the midst of the world."[9] Admitting the serious difficulties involved in comparing Christianity and Buddhism, rejecting all facile syncretism, and not at all indiscriminate in his approach to non-Christian religions, Merton still held for certain similarities between Christian love and Buddhist compassion, Christian original sin and Buddhist "ignorance," and Christ's *kenosis* and Buddhist "non-self."

Zen, for Merton, is neither a religion, nor a philosophy, nor an asceticism, nor even a mysticism in the Western sense. "Zen is consciousness unstructured by particular form or particular system, a trans-cultural, trans-religious, transformed consciousness. It is therefore in a sense 'void.' But it can shine through this or that system, religious or irreligious. . . ."[10] As noted above, however, Katz and others represent the counterposition to this view of Merton. For them, there is no such thing as consciousness unstructured by culture, tradition, religion, etc. Others maintain, moreover, that Merton depended far too much upon D. T. Suzuki for his interpretation of Zen. Unlike Suzuki, many Buddhists call Zen done without Buddhist faith *bompu* or "bastard" Zen.

Merton strongly rejects the contemporary view that all mystical experiences the world over are the same and that mystical experience is extrinsic to any particular religion. He repeatedly emphasizes the need for diverse religious traditions to shape and direct the mystical experience.

On the other hand, he found little, if any, difference in the essence of authentic religious experience. He provides a bridge between commentators like Huxley who hold that all mysticisms are the same and those like Zaehner who emphasize the radical differences with his view of "the fully integrated 'universal man' "[11] who takes on certain universal characteristics which do transcend in some ways any particular religion. As he says:

> Without asserting that there is complete unity of all religions at the "top," the transcendent or mystical level—that they all start from different dogmatic positions to "meet" at this summit—it is certainly true to say that even where there are irreconcilable differences in doctrine and in formulated beliefs, there may still be great similarities and analogies in the realm of religious experience. . . . Cultural and doctrinal differences must remain, but they do not invalidate the very real quality of existential likeness.[12]

Merton balanced a strong Christian identity with a genuine openness to all religious traditions, both East and West. He did not flinch from asserting that in terms of supernatural revelation, Christianity needs nothing from non-Christian religions. Yet, because of the Incarnation, he held that non-Christian religions are essential and necessary for the actual living out of the Christian mystery in history. "We must," he says, "contain all divided worlds in ourselves and transcend them in Christ."[13]

William Johnston

This Irish Jesuit has lived in Japan for over twenty-five years. Perhaps no Christian has written so lucidly and convincingly of the need for Christianity to take Buddhism, especially Zen, seriously than William Johnston. His background in the richly incarnational, kataphatic mysticism of St. Ignatius of Loyola has given him an appreciation for a mysticism of service and action that loves the world. His significant work on the dark, silent, imageless, apophatic mysticism of the fourteenth-century Christian mystical classic, *The Cloud of Unknowing,*[14] provided him with a Christian analogue for understanding the exotic world of Zen mysticism.

This gentle Irishman embodies, moreover, the ideal, contemporary Christian stance: a firm knowledge of and commitment to his Christian identity, an openness to and appreciation of the genuine religious values of the East, critical discernment, and lucid prose. If the noted Teilhard de Chardin integrated within his person the two currents of Christianity and evolution, Johnston has integrated Christianity and Zen. He lives what some commentators have asked for: a Christianity stretched beyond itself.[15]

According to Johnston, Christianity has much to learn from the East. Zen, especially, can give Christianity a much needed technology for deeper, richer, simpler prayer rooted in the body.[16] It can broaden and deepen Christianity, too, by aiding in the updating and in the transposing of the theology which underpins Christian mysticism. Just as the early Church both assimilated and rejected much from Jewish and Hellenistic cultures, contemporary Christianity must do the same with Oriental religions. Perhaps Christianity has failed in Asia because it refused to learn anything from local cultures and religions.

For Johnston, because the human psyche and its aspirations are the same the world over, our common human nature provides the basis for a Buddhist-Christian dialogue. Not philosophy and theology, but religious experience and the values of deep meditation, interiority, humility, compassion, non-violence, peace, and justice bind us together. The great religions can best meet at the level of dark faith and silent love, even when their beliefs are vastly different. As Johnston writes in his latest book:

> . . . any Buddhist-Christian dialogue must be based above all on religious experience and, ideally speaking, upon mysticism . . . the greatest union will be found when Buddhists and Christians meditate together. . . . The deepest union is found in pure and naked faith.[17]

Buddhists and Christians agree, however, that meditation, mysticism, and naked faith cannot be totally divorced from one's philosophy and theology of life. Although Johnston distinguishes naked faith from beliefs, he considers religious beliefs very important. There is a mutual interaction between naked faith and beliefs. It is impossible, therefore, to dissociate religious experience, mysticism, enlightenment, etc., from the religious beliefs and philosophy of life out of which they arise. Philosophy and theology nurture mystical experience, protect it, circumscribe it, and help it in the process of discerning genuine mysticism from aberration. Johnston argues, therefore, for a harmony between mysticism and reason. Mystical experience may be paradoxical and supra-conceptual, but it is not irrational and contradictory.

In addition, although Johnston calls attention to the striking similarity between the naked faith born from unrestricted love in the mystical heart of a Buddhist, Christian, or Hindu, he notes that this naked faith is not always the same. Furthermore, on the basis of his readings of Carl Jung, T.S. Eliot, and Dr. Takeo Doi, Johnston cautions against a slavish imitation of the East by the West. Both Zen and yoga have deep roots in Oriental traditions much different from the West. The power of these traditions upon the unconscious and archetypal patterns makes it imperative for the West to develop its own Zen and yoga.

"Mysticism is wisdom or knowledge that is found through love; it is loving knowledge,"[18] Johnston writes. Mysticism answers the call to unrestricted love which arises in the heart and goes on and on. Reaching out to foe and friend alike, this unrestricted love is universal. Incarnational in nature, it must love God and the world and be love in practical action. Authentic mysticism, therefore, looks upon the world with the eyes of love and compassion. Passing through the clouds of forgetting and unknowing, this unrestricted love brings enlightenment, supra-conceptual wisdom, and the naked, silent, dark faith found in every great religion. It fosters a realization of one's own poverty, folly, and emptiness. For Johnston, moreover, mysticism "is nothing less than a transformation of the whole person in preparation for that final transformation that takes place through death and resurrection."[19]

Johnston rejects the contemporary overemphasis upon the sometimes exotic and ecstatic side of mysticism. For him, it is frequently only "a deepened form of an ordinary human experience."[20] Every convinced believer is a mystic in embryo, for Christian mysticism is essentially an intensification of ordinary Christian life. In fact, because mysticism is frequently hidden and secret even to the one possessing it, Johnston believes that many people today from all walks of life have psyches permeated with *agape* and the silent, supra-conceptual wisdom of Zen enlightenment. For Johnston, genuine mysticism involves a "journey to the ordinary," a hallowing of daily life with the unspectacular loving mystical wisdom described by St. Paul in such banal terms in 1 Corinthians 13: "Love is patient, love is kind. It does not envy, it does not boast, it is not proud. It is not rude, it is not self-seeking, it is not easily angered, it keeps no record of wrongs. . . . Love bears all things, believes all things, hopes all things, endures all things."

Borrowing from St. Thomas Aquinas, Johnston defines mysticism philosophically as "the simple intuition of the truth."[21] Phenomenologically, however, it is the passage through the various layers of the psyche to the very core of the personality. "Vertical thinking" uncovers and reaches the deepest levels of the psyche beyond reason and discursive thinking. It brings and integrates the unconscious into consciousness. From this perspective, Johnston admits that psychedelic drugs may help a person to reach the deepest levels of the psyche. Unlike drug experiences, however, genuine mysticism promotes progress in psychic maturity, reform, conversion, and transformation. He also makes the useful distinction between "meditative states of consciousness" and "altered states of consciousness," between the authentic mystic in love with the mystery beyond consciousness and the explorer of consciousness interested only in the inner world.

Mysticism is a human experience, for Johnston, not limited to any one religion. Anyone who is faithful to what Lonergan calls "the transcendental precepts," our basic human drives to be attentive, intelligent, reasonable, responsible, committed, and in love, progresses toward authenticity and self-transcendence. What all religions have in common is the search for fulfillment, authenticity, and self-realization. In fact, Johnston holds for a graced, supernatural mysticism in non-Christian religions, although he concedes that not all mysticism is graced.

For Johnston, therefore, "mysticism which arises from, and culminates in, love of God in Christ is Christian; that which does not (but yet remains a simple intuition of the truth) is non-Christian."[22] It is difficult, therefore, to distinguish Christian from non-Christian mysticism, except by theological definition. Johnston says, for example, that Zen and Christian mysticism belong together philosophically and phenomenologically, but not theologically. On the other hand, they are not exactly the same even phenomenologically. Zen involves "meditation without an object"; Christianity, "meditation without a subject." It does make some difference phenomenologically if God disappears during meditation and only the "I" remains, or if the "I" disappears and only God remains.[23]

Zen meditation, according to Johnston, is "a process of unification in which the whole personality is harmonized in a oneness which reaches its climax with a complete absence of subject-object consciousness in satori."[24] The Zen contemplative sits in the lotus position, gathers energy in the *hara* (a point two inches below the navel), breathes deeply and rhythmically, empties the mind, and forgets the ego. The latter is aided either by counting one's breathing or by focusing upon a *koan*. The *koan* is a paradox (e.g., "What was your original face before you were born?") embodying Buddhist wisdom which prevents discursive reasoning. It can be solved only when the Zen contemplative identifies with the *koan*, becomes the *koan*, so that the answer arises from the deepest depths of her being.

These practices bring about *sanmai*, a state of deep concentration which gradually unifies the contemplative's personality. The sense of one's own ego diminishes, and one begins to see all things in their essential nudity. The Zennist becomes increasingly present to all reality, to the fact that things *are*, but this presence is accomplished with great emotional detachment.

These periods of concentration usually bring about periods of hallucinations, *makyo*, the world of the devil. Preconscious, subconscious, unconscious, and unintegrated elements of the psyche arise into consciousness to torture, tempt, seduce, harass, or to lead the Zennist astray. The Zennist must ignore this, reveal it to the Zen master, be still, and let these inner beasts die. As Johnston notes, the Zennist during this period must pass through the "great doubt," or some psychotic phase similar to the Christian dark night of the soul, to reach enlightenment.

Satori, or enlightenment, frequently occurs outside of meditation. A falling leaf, the sound of the temple gong, a blow from the Zen master—any of these may trigger an enlightenment experience of varying quality and depth. The Zennist experiences the dissolution of the great doubt. His skull seems to shatter like an ice castle. Calm, joy, interior freedom, and a unified personality follow. The contemplative's mind becomes identified with and sees into the very essence of all things.

An enlightened Zen master must sanction the disciple's enlightenment. Because of the deep master-disciple relationship in the Zen tradition, the master intuitively knows if and when the disciple is enlightened. *Inka,* or confirmation of enlightenment, is an intrinsic element of the enlightenment experience in this tradition. To find, therefore, a genuinely enlightened Zen master is of crucial importance in the contemporary Zen scene.

Johnston emphasizes that Zen hinders the rational mind in order to open up the deepest subliminal layers of the psyche. Enlightenment renders the unconscious conscious. The Zen contemplative, however, does not see different things, but all things differently through the enlightened inner eye of love. Through the loss of the daily "I," moreover, the true, universal, poetic self, the "big ego," the "true self" is born. Such is the healing power and wholeness conferred by Zen.

Although the Zennist experiences undifferentiated unity during enlightenment (his unity with all things and the unity of all things with him), this differs dramatically from the pure blank of yogic consciousness. The Zennist, moreover, must use monist language to describe the experience, but experientially he sees that everything is one, yet not one. The "oneness" and the "suchness" of all reality become luminous to each other. For Johnston, "monism reminds Christianity of the unity of all things and our oneness with God."[25]

Zen enlightenment, however, does not terminate in the undifferentiated consciousness of one's unity with all things. A loving and compassionate consciousness which seeks to save all sentient beings flows from Zen enlightenment. The Zen seeker who left all things to follow the "tracks of the ox,"[26] once enlightened, returns to the market-place as the wise old man for a life of service through contemplation-in-action. The wise old man may even be assassinated because of his enlightened commitment to truth, justice, and peace.

Johnston contends that Christianity is founded on the trinitarian mystical experiences of the crucified and risen Christ. Christianity, however, does not emphasize a technically developed mysticism to the extent Buddhism does. True Christian enlightenment comes only after death, and the Church canonizes saints for their heroic

charity, not their mysticism. To be sure, Johnston stresses the implicitly mystical dimension of Christian charity and the variety of ways
in which it can be fostered. On the other hand, he seems to hold that
Christian contemplative prayer is one of the best means to heroic
charity.

The Christian mystical journey usually begins with active meditation upon the Scriptures. One remembers and ponders the great
Christian mysteries to interiorize them. This discursive activity frequently contains or gives way to an affective stage in which one feels
differently about oneself, others, Christ, and God. As this discursive-
affective prayer simplifies, the person may be able to rest in one
thought or emotion. The prayer of simplicity, or "acquired contemplation," is rich in silence and interior tasting.

Mystical contemplation, in the strict sense, begins with the
prayer of quiet, the experience of being grasped by the living flame of
love at the core of one's being. One rests simply and silently in the
presence of Something or Someone. As Johnston writes: "The sense
of presence is . . . one of the chief characteristics of Christian mysticism."[27] This loving awareness is both a rich emptiness and the
consoling fullness of supra-conceptual wisdom. Although distractions and a roving imagination frequently plague this prayer, the
person experiences peace, silence, and unification at the deepest
levels. The contemplative may reach a point where this experience
becomes an habitually present state.

As the living flame of love takes deeper hold, however, the
contemplative experiences the pain of the mystical process of becoming one with God and self. The sins of one's past life, or other forms
of psychic debris, may arise to torture and to purify. One may then
experience oneself as a "lump of sin" through frequent and acute
encounters with the "shadow." Eventually the purifying and transforming pain of one's distance from God and one's inability to love
as much as one is loved dominates. Mystical prayer stirs the deepest
levels of the psyche, levels usually dormant. Johnston indicates that
these "nights" purify, heal, and transform both the personal and
collective unconscious dimensions of the psyche.

The purification process from the living flame of love enables
even deeper, simpler prayer. The contemplative now moves to the
prayer of union. Undistracted prayer with all of the person's powers

centered on God in the so-called "sleep of the faculties" characterizes this prayer. The intense concentration which unites all levels of psychic life may result in sudden, violent ecstasies and raptures. During these irresistible transports of the human spirit, the senses cease to act, the bodily limbs become immobile, breathing and heartbeat dramatically diminish, and the body's heat is lowered.

Although Johnston agrees with those authors who do not consider ecstasy essential for mystical ascent, he underscores its great significance. To be taken out of one's self to a new level of consciousness is a step toward a more universal and cosmic form of consciousness. Mystical ecstasy foreshadows both the ecstasy of death and life in the risen body. Moreover, almost all of the great Christian mystics experienced ecstasies and raptures.

The final mystical state is transforming union, or mystical marriage. The contemplative becomes God by participation, identified with God through love, yet separate in nature and personality. God and the contemplative truly become one, yet remain two. Unlike Zen, this union of love beyond subject and object is one of differentiated unity, for, as Johnston notes, "In the Hebrew-Christian tradition *the true self is essentially relational.*"[28] The Persons in the Trinity are three, yet one, and mutually indwell in each other. The contemplative and God are two, yet one, and mutually indwell in each other. And as we saw in the Underhill section, this stage is also characterized by "spiritual fecundity," a marriage with the God of love that results in compassion and love for the world which parallels Zen's "return to the market-place."

The enlightened love of both the desert-solitary and the active person serves the world. The desert-solitary's enlightened love is already a "return to the market-place," for it unites through compassion the solitary to the poor, needy, and underprivileged. There is a genuine union with the world effected through mystical union with God. The effective life-giving and personalizing energy from the desert-solitary humanizes the world in a way that unenlightened, unconverted social activism can never do.

Frequently, however, mystical love overflows into direct service to humanity. Experiencing the presence and the working of the Spirit of Love within them, the great contemplative-actives unite compassion and love with political insight, pragmatic concerns, and economic progress. Or one may reach enlightenment and union with God through this pragmatic concern for the world and humanity. When Mother Teresa, for example, experiences Christ by touching the poor, "this union or solidarity with the poor and oppressed is of the very essence of Christian mysticism."[29]

For Johnston, Zen and Christian contemplation have much in common. Both make use of "vertical meditation" which results in seeing into one's nature and an experience beyond subject and object. Both require walking a path of naked faith filled with the "nights" of doubt and anguish. Both must deal with the temptations, delusions, and illusions which arise when the deep levels of the psyche are disturbed.

The vertical meditation of both traditions deepens personality, strengthens convictions, results in serene detachment, aids interior liberty, and promotes psychic growth and emotional maturity. The Eastern emphasis upon the non-self, non-attachment, and the perfect wisdom of Nothingness beyond subject and object parallels Christ's *kenosis* and the Christian contemplative's self-emptying to cling to a God found only in the darkness, emptiness, and the obscurity of the cloud of unknowing. Johnston insists, however, that Zen and Christianity differ experimentally and not only in the way they interpret their experiences. The Zen experience of an enlightenment beyond subject and object in undifferentiated unity is not the same as the Christian experience of a love identification beyond subject and object in differentiated unity.[30]

Johnston has made a significant contribution to the difficult problem of reconciling an authentic apophatic mysticism with a Christianity inextricably bound to the person of Jesus Christ. On the practical level, Johnston points out that the dark, silent, apophatic mysticism of *The Cloud of Unknowing* is penetrated with a personal love for the man Jesus. On the theoretical level, Johnston stresses that the universal, cosmic, and risen Christ cannot be represented or known adequately in words, images, and thoughts. The universal, cosmic, risen Christ buried deep in the human heart and coextensive with the universe, as Teilhard held, is best known as a presence in the darkness, silence, and void of apophatic emptiness.

The Christian contemplative best experiences the presence of this Christ within by becoming, by being transformed into, and identifying with Christ. To say with St. Paul, "I live, not I, but Christ lives in me," is to have had one's "mystical senses" fully transformed. There is a seeing without seeing, a hearing without hearing, a touching without touching, a tasting without tasting, and a smelling without smelling which takes the Christian contemplative far beyond any objective meditation on the person of Christ. Both in silent contemplation and in daily life, moreover, the contemplative must imitate Christ's radical and complete self-emptying.

Jesus' own "I am" expressed perfect enlightenment, in words not from the empirical ego. This is the "I" of the eternal Word, Buddhism's "big self," and "the very ground of being, the heart of the universe, the true self which arises in the depths and overwhelms everything."[31] Because Christ is none other than the true self of the human race, the archetypal man, he is the final Word which arises in the human heart and which grounds all other mystical words which arise from mystical interiority.

The person who contemplates, according to Johnston, becomes psychosomatically different from the person who does not. Vertical thinking transforms the entire body-person by anchoring the living flame of love more deeply. It purifies and transforms all levels of the psyche, especially the unconscious, and roots faith, hope, and love in the contemplative's very guts. Meditation, however, is not necessarily therapeutic. The inner journey may disturb elements in the psyche which the contemplative cannot control. On the other hand, the experience of being loved and the energy released during contemplation always get at the roots of pride and today's sense of meaninglessness. It nurtures, then, both therapeutic and "deeper healing."

Johnston also emphasizes the cosmic dimension and significance of the contemplative's body. The Zen monk "sits" for the universe; the Christian contemplative is one with the universal, cosmic Christ. Their contemplative activity releases cosmic energy, an energy which heals, personalizes, and transforms the universe. By adumbrating the cosmic resurrection at the end of the world, the mystic, for Johnston, is the most influential person in the world.

Deep contemplation must always involve more than technique. What makes contemplation religious or non-religious is one's sense of values and one's motivation. Although Johnston insists that one's ultimate concern does not have to be explicitly religious, he distinguishes contemplation done for the development of human potential from that done with faith, hope, and love. In practice, however, the dividing line may be rather blurred. Still, unless the awareness exercises of the East are done in faith, hope, and love, there is no authentic mysticism. Even deep intellectual and moral conversion is not mystical, unless permeated with love. Johnston postulates that Aldous Huxley, despite his contemplation and detachment, got nowhere because of his lack of faith. Some commentators agree with Johnston that the self-*realization* wrought in authentic mystical self-transcendence in faith, hope and love—regardless of the technique used—must be distinguished from a self-*actualization* wrought through techniques to develop human potential.[32]

Although Johnston argues for the incorporation of Eastern contemplation techniques into Christian prayer, he finds many parallels to Zen in Christianity. Christianity, for example, has its own *koans,* meta-rational puzzles, which can only be solved through becoming more deeply one with Christ. The crucifix, the risen Body, the Trinity, the God-man, the Eucharist, etc., are only a few examples. The rosary, Gregorian Chant, the Jesus Prayer, ejaculatory prayers, etc., all make use of our basic psychosomatic rhythm to promote deep, silent mystical prayer. Prayer before the Blessed Sacrament is a type of yoga which fixes the person's attention on one point, the vigil light, or the tabernacle. The contemplative reading of the Bible and various devotions which develop refined and delicate religious feelings can also be ways to the deepest mystical levels.

Because of the purifying quality of deep contemplation, it frequently leads to deeply intimate, non-clinging interpersonal relationships, or mystical friendships. These extraordinary friendships involve not only love for another person, but also love for humanity and for God. The relationship between the master and disciple may be an example of a mystical friendship founded on the religious experience of two people in love without reserve. In fact, Johnston stresses the importance of a community of love, faith, and commitment for the development of genuine mysticism.

While ongoing mystical love preserves, transforms, and transfigures biological, romantic, and devotional love, these three loves are also, perhaps, the most human roads to eventual contemplation, enlightenment, and union. When faithful to the *deepest* dynamisms of these three loves, the person becomes present to Christ as a third party, and experiences mystical love and enlightenment.

A new and important partner in the Buddhist-Christian dialogue must be today's scientists interested in altered states of consciousness. And as contemplation and mysticism provide an excellent basis for the Buddhist-Christian dialogue, they can also serve for the religious-scientific dialogue. With a view similar to Carl Albrecht's, Johnston emphasizes that mysticism will always be a love affair with wisdom about which theologians may stutter. It contains a religious core beyond science's ken. Because of the psychological, physiological, and neurological basis of mysticism, however, science has much to say about and much to contribute concerning the psychosomatic and neurological repercussions of this love affair. In short, the East-West dialogue, psychoanalysis, the study of brain-waves, biofeedback, etc., must all contribute to the updating of the new science of mysticism.

In order to dialogue with the East, the West must rethink its theology in the light of mystical experience. Ideally speaking, theology should arise out of and lead back into mystical experience. This was so in earlier ages of the Church when living spiritually and theological speculation nourished each other.

Contemporary Christian theology, for Johnston, must reflect upon the mystical experience of Jesus, the disciples, mystics living and dead, and the entire Christian community. Reflection upon mystical experience and conversion can provide the foundation for a future Christian theology able to dialogue with the East. Johnston sees, moreover, in Bernard Lonergan's transcendental method the common ground for a foundational theology between East and West. Both East and West must be attentive, intelligent, reasonable, responsible, and committed.

Summary

Both Merton and Johnston have focused attention upon the values of Eastern religions for Christianity and the need for genuine dialogue based upon mystical experience. Both delineate mysticism as a way of life irreducible to ecstatic experience. They also emphasize Zen's special ability to destroy illusion, allow the "transcendental unconscious" to enter consciousness, promote healing, and aid the "big Self" to come forth. Although Merton and Johnston contend that not all mysticisms are the same, they point out the similarities and parallels of the "fully integrated universal man" of any world religion.

Merton holds that Zen is a "wisdom-intuition" open to its sublation into Christianity. Johnston treats Zen as a graced mysticism which moves from concentration upon one's breathing or a *koan,* to deep levels of concentration, to wrestling with *makyo,* to an enlightenment which must be sanctioned and which leads to compassion. He sees its culmination in an undifferentiated unity in which all is somehow one, but not one. Johnston also shows how the Zen movement parallels the classical Christian stages of mystical ascent. For Johnston, Christianity is based on the trinitarian mysticism of Jesus Christ. He is especially good at delineating the naked faith, the loving knowledge, the psychosomatic effects, and the deeply human qualities of "vertical meditation."

Like Katz and others, he refuses to separate mysticism from its traditions, culture, and reason. He emphasizes both the indirectly and the directly apostolic values of genuine mysticism. He appeals for a new science of mysticism based upon the contemporary sciences and for a new mystical theology which reflects upon conversion and mystical experience. For Johnston, service, devotion, spiritual reading, friendship, human love, etc., may all lead to mysticism which is a universal phenomenon not reserved for an elite. It is essentially deeply human life.

That not all are sanguine about Christianity's Eastern turn will be clear from the next section which deals with those critical of this positive evaluation of Eastern mystical traditions.

7
Turning East Criticized

Pierre Teilhard de Chardin

This author offers more than a counterpoint to the previous section on Christianity's interest in Eastern mysticisms. Few contemporary writers have grasped the importance of mysticism and spirituality for the twentieth century with such depth as this Jesuit priest, paleontologist, world traveler, poet, visionary, and mystic. "Mysticism is the Science of Sciences," he writes, "the great science and the great art, the only power capable of synthesizing the riches accumulated by other forms of human activity."[1]

Teilhard provides a strong counterpoint to Merton because of his uncompromising acceptance of evolution, science, technology, and contemporary life in general. He loudly rejected the nostalgic view of those desiring to return to an alleged golden age during which the human person was supposedly more unified with himself and nature. His goal was to Christify evolution, to reconcile and unite science and Christianity. And he succeeded by blending in his own person a passionate love for the world and for God. He was convinced that

> the mystical vibration is inseparable from the scientific vibration: To read the Secret of the Real ... to find its source: the scientist's quest, however positivisitic he may claim it to be, is coloured or haloed—or rather is invincibly animated, fundamentally—by a mystical hope.[2]

On the other hand, Teilhard's universe formed a unity only in Christ. "The true mystical science [is] the science of Christ through all things."[3]

Science, religion, and mysticism are different aspects of the one person's deep aspirations for unity. Ultimately, they have the same goal: surrender to what is greater than the human person. "All human effort," for Teilhard, "whether religious or scientific, whether action or contemplation, must finally lead to worship, adoration and ecstasy."[4]

From the data of both the experimental sciences and Christian revelation, therefore, Teilhard attempted a "hyperphysics," an "ultraphysics," a new anthropology, which grasped all things in their cosmic matrix. The necessary reflection upon scientific data takes the person only so far. Faith is ultimately necessary to achieve an intellectual synthesis.

Faith and science need each other to be able to see the Real. Seeing was essential for Teilhard, because "to see is really to become more ... a deeper vision is really fuller being."[5] His seeing, his intellectual synthesis, therefore, combined the inner sight of the mystical gift of faith with the outer study of scientific phenomena. He was convinced that scientific thought and religious faith have to be in much closer contact for a converging vision to emerge.

Because Marxism served and fostered science, evolution, and humanism, it fascinated Teilhard. He described it as a "youthful form of religion," a religion which imparted a deep taste for the human and a "sense of the earth." Lacking a genuine grasp of transcendence, immortality, and personhood, it left humankind feeling incomplete and insecure. In addition, Teilhard rightly criticized Marxism for its internationalization of hatred, for its demolition of sympathy, compassion, and love as the only authentic basis for humanism.

Overly enthusiastic and uncritical admirers of Eastern religions will find in Teilhard an exceptionally strong repudiation of the turn toward the East. He had traveled to Asia with great hopes, but had been quickly disappointed. Although drawn by the universalistic and cosmic view of Buddhism, he found in its mysticism an unwillingness and a basic inability to incorporate contemporary science, evolution,

and other Western ideas. In fact, for Teilhard, Buddhism seemed to
deny them outright. Even more to the point, he noted,

> it is in the particular, *specific* nature of Buddhist detach-
> ment that there lies the weakness and the (at least logical)
> danger of Eastern religions. The Buddhist *denies* himself in
> order to kill desire (he *does not believe* in the value of
> *being*).[6]

Because of Hinduism's stress upon passivity and detachment, it
fared no better in Teilhard's assessment. Hinduism has not and could
not build a better world. It, too, denied evolution. Even more
trenchantly, Teilhard wrote: "If you only knew how much I mistrust
Hindu mysticism—it is based not on union, which generates love,
but on identification, which excludes love."[7] For Teilhard, Hinduism
kills love in two ways. It proclaims an impersonal Absolute and the
final merging and dissolution of everything finite in this Impersonal.

Ironically, Teilhard held that the East could not save the West
from materialism, for Eastern pantheism had already given in to the
temptation to worship nature and matter. "In reality," for both
Hinduism and Buddhism, "everything is *materialized.* . . . *Life is
understood and experienced as a function of matter.*"[8] These religions
had actually drugged humanity with nature.

Although Teilhard praised Islam for its early recognition of
man's close unity with nature and for the Sufi experience of oneness,
he dismissed Islam as "a backward-looking revival of Judaism"
which "offers itself today as a principle of fixation and stagnation."[9]
Islam, Hinduism, Buddhism, Taoism, and Confucianism, moreover,
are utterly irreconcilable with contemporary knowledge and progress. The genuinely contemporary Muslim, Hindu, Buddhist, Taoist,
or Confucian necessarily lives a schizophrenic interior life.

The East, on the other hand, utterly fascinated Teilhard because
of its emphasis upon the universe's ultimate unity. The living currents of faith there stirred deeply his own personal inclinations
toward pantheism. He had confessed, in fact, to being a "naturally
pantheistic soul." In the Egyptian desert, Teilhard experienced radically the temptation of matter:

And then all my sensibility became alert, as though at the
approach of a god of easy-won happiness and intoxication;
for there lay matter, and matter was calling me. To me in
my turn, as to all the sons of man, it was speaking as every
generation hears it speak; it was begging me to surrender
myself unreservedly to it, and to worship it.[10]

This all-embracing unitive experience of the fundamental oneness of all phenomena had mesmerized Teilhard. On the other hand,
he vigorously repudiated the appeal of matter and the earth. He saw
in what he called monistic, pagan, natural, immanent pantheism the
ultimate trap: escape from evolution's true call to ascend by fusing
with and dissolving into nature. This was a false pantheism of
descent, a mysticism which took the person in the wrong direction.
He decided, therefore, to renew his effort, to "reverse my course and
ascend."

Teilhard draws a sharp distinction between "pagan" and
"Christian pantheism." Pagan pantheism reverses the direction of
evolution toward greater interiority, heightened complexity, and
concentration. It is a pantheism of relaxation and diffusion. The
pagan mystic loses his consciousness and eventually his very person.
This mysticism operates without love and culminates in an identification of all things with the Absolute. It proclaims that God is All.
Pagan pantheism, moreover, allows only a "communion with the
earth."

Christian pantheism, on the other hand, promotes a communion
with God through the earth. It preserves evolution's upward thrust
toward greater complexity, consciousness, and personhood. Centered
on an ultra-personal God and powered by genuine love, this mysticism through an increased tension culminates in a union which
confirms and deepens the identity of each individual element. It is a
mysticism of differentiated unity in which God is All in all.

The distinction between the "Road of the East" and the "Road
of the West" is a fundamental orientation of Teilhard's thought.
Both are roads to ultimate unity. The "Road of the East," however,
opposes totally the Absolute and the many. This path promotes
unity by negating or eliminating all plurality. The return to original
unity takes place by way of detachment, simplification, "impoverish-

ment," identification, and the fusion of all elements. This dehumanizing spirituality maintains an exclusively vertical orientation between the person and the Absolute. It emphasizes contemplation and contemplation alone. Preaching the radical emptiness of the experimental universe, this mysticism of identification kills all constructive activity. Evading life and ultimately denying the reality of visible reality, it "renounces earth, its passions and cares, and the effort it demands."[11] De-differentiation and de-personalization result from this loveless mysticism.

Teilhard also distinguished three types of Eastern spiritualities. The Indian type finds God and the invisible more evident than the world and the visible. Its paradigm is monism and its "emptiness-inebriation." The Chinese type is both humanistic and naturalistic. The tangible and visible take precedence. The Japanese type is essentially a social mysticism, "an heroic sense of the collective." Although each of these spiritualities solves in a particular way the human problem of relating to God, the world, and others, what is lacking is an overall synthesis.

The "Road of the West," on the other hand, *progresses* to an ultimate unity brought about by convergence, complexification, enrichment, and differentiation. It encompasses both detachment and attachment, unity and differentiation, contemplation and action. Synthesizing the person's vertical thrust toward God and his horizontal thrust toward others and the world, this diagonal thrust, or *via media,* is a mysticism of union with the ultimate personal Center in which the many are transformed and fulfilled. This is a mysticism which loves others and the world in God and vice versa.

Teilhard was convinced that "Christianity alone . . . saves . . . the essential aspiration of all mysticism: *to be united* (that is, to become the other) *while remaining oneself.*"[12] Because "Christian mysticism extracts *all* that is sweetest and strongest circulating in all the human mysticisms, though without absorbing their evil or suspect elements,"[13] Christianity is the major axis for the development of the mysticism and religion of the future. It alone provides the strength necessary for all creation to transcend itself in God and yet not to lose its identity through pantheistic dissolution in God. As Teilhard says: *"We can lose ourselves in God by prolonging the most individual characteristics of being far beyond themselves."*[14] Only

Christianity, therefore, preserves the human desire for God, others, and the earth without weakening or eliminating any of these three aspects.

To equate the "Road of the West" with Christianity as it currently exists, however, would be a serious misunderstanding of Teilhard. He sought a "Christianity which surpasses itself," one which faithfully extends itself to its utmost limit, one free from its specifically Mediterranean trappings. He seriously questioned, moreover, whether contemporary Christianity was sufficient for today's world. In short, he was searching for a new mysticism, for a transformed Christianity which loved evolution. Teilhard wanted a mysticism which could take up and further energize the dynamism of the contemporary world by fostering a "taste for life" and imparting the meaning necessary for further evolution. This new mysticism must transform the " 'God of the Gospel' into the 'God of Evolution'—a transformation without deformation."[15]

Taking into account the complementary insights of other faiths, this new mysticism must generate and promote the psychic energy required for evolution's increasingly greater unity and convergence. Only a genuine Christian pantheism can ultimately satisfy humanity's pluralistic and monistic desires and tendencies. The human person's radical desire for the All and the unifying experience of cosmic consciousness is a paradigm of a "natural mysticism of which Christian mysticism can only be a sublimation and crowning peak."[16] Although Teilhard judged Eastern pantheisms insufficient, he did not really reject them. He saw their fulfillment in Christian personalism. His Christian pantheism takes into account that "the Universe flows . . . in the direction of 'ever greater order and consciousness' . . . a superior and synthetic form of 'mysticism' in which the strengths and seductions of Oriental 'pantheism' and Christian personalism converge and culminate."[17] Only in a person-centered, theistic mysticism of unifying and differentiating love could monistic pantheism, for Teilhard, find its true transformation, goal, and fulfillment.

"Pagan" or "natural" mysticism, the appeal of matter, earth, and the cosmos found in pantheistic monism, strongly attracted Teilhard for most of his life. "And why, indeed, should I not worship it, the stable, the great, the rich, the mother, the divine? Is not matter, in its own way, eternal and immense?"[18] he questioned. But Teilhard held this attraction in tension with a mysticism penetrated with personal love. He confessed: "At no moment in my life, have I found the least difficulty in speaking to God as to a Supreme Some One."[19]

That many today have ceased to believe in a personal God is the root of contemporary malaise, for Teilhard. To believe in the universe, the oneness of all things, an ultimate impersonal force in which the human personality is absorbed and lost, vitiates evolution's thrust toward a personal and personalizing universe. Teilhard saw the universe evolving from and toward a "hyper-personal God," an "ultra-personal Center." Because the fully evolved and transformed universe was to be a "theosphere of Love" in which God would be "All in all," only an "amorization" process could keep evolution on course. Love dies, however, in the presence of an impersonal Absolute. Hence, the "way of the East" deprives evolution of its highest form of energy: love.

Teilhard expressly denied that Buddhist compassion or the love emphasized between God and man in the Hindu *bhakti* tradition was the equivalent of Christian love. Buddhist compassion ultimately surrenders to undifferentiated unity with the Ultimate; hence, compassion dissolves into "relaxation." *Bhakti* pays no attention to others, evolution, and the world. Only Christian love is capable of a "neo-love" which integrates love of God, others, and a world in evolution. Only Christian love possesses the dynamic, transforming quality which unites persons in their "irreplaceable and incommunicable essence" with each other and with the personal God of Love. Teilhard wrote: "If man is to be fully himself and fully living, he must, (1) be centered upon himself; (2) be 'de-centered' upon 'the other'; (3) be supercentered upon a being greater than himself."[20] Christian mysticism is unique, therefore, in transforming and fulfilling the person's need for self-identity, for social identity, and for an identity in God. It is the highest type of mysticism, a mysticism of union with differentiation.

The mystical illusion, for Teilhard, "pretends to Union and Presence *independently of Time* and Evolution . . . as if the contact with God could be achieved without the Evolution of Consciousness—from the beginning."[21] Teilhard's mystical vision embraced, therefore, a universal, personal, and evolutionary world converging on a personal Center. The world's great religions are moving toward greater unification with a certain irreversibility. These religions are converging, however, around Christianity as their principal "axis." Because the convergence of all religions occurs by way of a concurrent process of differentiation and unification, Teilhard rejected both the view of a "common core" behind all religions and also the view of syncretism. His "new mysticism of convergence" does not show itself in "the sterile and conservative ecumenism of a 'common ground' but [in] the creative ecumenism of a 'convergence' . . . on a common ideal."[22] Moreover, "in reality, the true Christian ideal is 'integralism,' namely the extension of the Christian directives to all the resources contained in the world."[23] This is, moreover, a new synthesis, and not syncretism.

Above all, however, Teilhard's mysticism was "the science of Christ running through all things."[24] Concerning his overall mystical synthesis, Teilhard wrote:

> I believe that the universe is an evolution. I believe that evolution proceeds towards spirit. I believe that in man, spirit is fully realized in person. I believe that the supremely personal is the Universal Christ.[25]

In the light of the Christian teaching on creation and incarnation, Teilhard mystically viewed the entire evolution of the cosmos, cosmogenesis, as a real Christogenesis, the becoming of the cosmic Christ. At point Alpha, God created out of nothing and initiated an evolutionary process of unification, complexification, and becoming-more. With complexification comes increased interiority, consciousness, and tension. Like a coiled helix, circling in ever-decreasing circles in increasing tension, cosmogenesis embraces biogenesis, the evolution of life, and anthropogenesis, the evolution of man.

Man, for Teilhard, is the spearhead of evolution. In man, evolution becomes self-conscious and produces the noosphere, a layer of thought in the evolutionary process. Important for understanding Teilhard is his view that man evolves not only as an individual with increasing interiority, but also as a social being. As anthropogenesis proceeds, heightened forms of socialization appear.

Because love is the key energy in cosmogenesis, Christianity, as a "phylum of love," has a major role in the universe's evolution. Love binds the individual elements in the universe to each other and to the universe's personal Center. This love confirms the identity of each element but transforms them into a synthesis of ever-greater interiority and unity. At point Omega, the point of cosmic convergence, evolution ecstatically surrenders to God's final transformation process. At Omega, God becomes All in all in a "theosphere of love."

The person of Jesus Christ is, for Teilhard, the axis of evolution. He called Christ the "Evolver." His own bodily resurrection prefigures the universe's final transformation into God which is, at the same time, his own risen, cosmic body. Although Teilhard never lost sight of the man Jesus and never eliminated the necessary distinction between nature and grace, he emphasized the universal, cosmic Christ, "the spearhead of monotheism . . . incommensurable with any prophet or Buddha."[26] He held, therefore, for some sort of natural identity of Christ and the universe. Cosmogenesis, the evolution of the universe, was radically a Christogenesis, the evolution of the universal and cosmic Christ. He had proclaimed that "*Jesus must be loved as a world.*"[27] The universal and cosmic Christ holds all things together, for Teilhard. Because of Christogenesis, we receive a share in the divine life through Christ by becoming one Christ, but with a transformation and confirmation of our own identity, not its loss in mystical dissolution. With good reason, commentators have called Teilhard's Christo-cosmic vision, his "Christian pantheism," a "Christo-monism," a "pan-Christic monism" or simply a "pan-Christism." For Teilhard, "it is *Christ whom we make or whom we undergo in all things.*"[28]

Teilhard's divine milieu, which he first called a "mystical milieu," is essentially a Christic milieu. He wrote:

> At the heart of the universe, each soul exists for God, in our Lord. But all reality, even material reality, around each one of us, exists for our souls. Hence, all sensible reality, around each one of us, exists, through our souls, for God in our Lord.[29]

Everything the person does and undergoes, therefore, contributes to cosmogenesis and Christogenesis. Teilhard's mystical seeking of God in all things emphasizes that all of human life must be and can be sanctified. To touch God in all things, we must work, act, develop our talents and abilities, and throw ourselves without reserve into the building of a better world. The exact fulfillment of the least of our obligations, for Teilhard, is a way of being a living extension of the incarnation.

To be a person of action, however, requires great detachment. Work means overcoming inertia, forgetting oneself, overcoming the temptation to seek only personal honor, and creative self-transcendence in bringing about the divine milieu. True attachment to the world means divinizing the world in Jesus Christ. It demands genuine Christian detachment and going to the full limits of one's humanity.

Teilhard also emphasized a mystical surrender to human passivities, to those things which we undergo. Much of our life is a gift to which we must surrender. It is easy to surrender to the "passivities of growth," those pleasant and friendly forces which promote our growth. There are, however, also "passivities of diminishment," what others do to us, accidents, bad fortune, obstacles, natural failings, personal limitations, disease, and death. Although God must empty us in order to fill us with Himself, Teilhard states:

> I can only unite myself to the will of God (as endured passively) *when all my strength is spent,* at the point where my activity, extended and straining towards betterment (understood in ordinary human terms), finds itself continually counter-weighted by forces tending to halt me or overwhelm me.[30]

Teilhard viewed attachment and detachment as the two phases of life's basic rhythm. I must develop myself in order to be myself, but I must also surrender to diminishment in order to be in another. The paradigm of genuine Christian attachment and detachment is the crucified Christ, "the symbol and the reality of the immense labour of the centuries which has, little by little, raised up the created spirit and brought it back to the depths of the divine *milieu.*"[31]

It would be a mistake, therefore, to see Teilhard's mysticism exclusively as a mysticism of action. Surrender to the passivities of growth and diminishment is also an essential aspect of the divine milieu. Teilhard found, moreover, in the strictly contemplative life a "wonderful power of condensing the divine in all around us." [32] The contemplative becomes an evolutionary force, an actual axis of evolution, because of the purity, "the rectitude and the impulse introduced into our lives by the love of God sought in and above everything."[33] The contemplative's operative faith consecrates the world and her fidelity communicates with it.

Although Teilhard places great emphasis upon the dignity of the individual as a particular center of divinization, his mysticism is also radically social. He says: "The only subject ultimately capable of mystical transformation is the whole group of mankind forming a single body and a single soul in charity."[34] Christian love of neighbor is likewise an evolutionary energy which confirms the identity of another and unites all in such wise that "only one man will be saved: Christ, the head and living summary of humanity."[35] Teilhard's Christian mysticism loves God, the world, and others in Christ through whom God is becoming All in all.

Many have praised Teilhard for his mysticism centered on the consuming fire of divine love, global in intent, Christocentric and Theocentric, creatively expressed in evolutionary terms, and looking toward a future mysticism which synthesizes, yet transcends, the distinctions between East and West. One can ask, however, whether his vision is sufficiently Trinitarian. In his search for a new mysticism capable of sustaining the dynamism of contemporary man, did Teilhard too summarily dismiss the richness of the Christian mystical tradition to which he owes such a debt?

Teilhard's cosmic and increasingly ecumenical interests encouraged him to integrate Eastern mysticisms into his synthesis. But his emphatically Christian personalism caused him to repudiate other aspects of Eastern religions. One may agree with Ursula King, however, that Teilhard had greatly underestimated the power of Eastern religions to adapt themselves to the demands of the contemporary world. Although Teilhard had a greater interest and knowledge of many facets of Eastern thought than one suspects by reading

his writings, one can still say that he seriously misjudged the importance the East would have on Western mystical ideas, practices, self-
assessment, and orientation.

Ursula King has also shown that Teilhard's sharp distinction
between the "Road of the East" and the "Road of the West" is more
typological, evaluative, heuristic, and theoretical than a description
of what actually exists in practice. "Understood literally rather than
typologically, they are often inaccurate, harsh, and unjust,"[36] King
notes. Although Christianity still has much to learn from, can be
greatly enriched by, and itself has much to contribute to the East,
there may be more than a germ of truth in Teilhard's view that:

> . . . if the religions of India are less negative than I said,
> that fact does not essentially affect my thesis, the purpose
> of which is above all to distinguish "two essential types" of
> possible mysticisms. It would be quite extraordinary, I
> admit, for either of these types to be met anywhere in the
> *pure state*. . . . I still believe that, *logically*, Eastern religions
> and contemplation kill action. . . .[37]

In view of Teilhard's remarkable synthesis of a personal God,
other persons, the world, science, evolution, the East, and Christianity in a new mysticism which he essentially lived, it is distressing that
many contemporary commentators on mysticism neglect him in
their studies. Can it be that Teilhard's uncompromisingly radical
Christian personalism offers too potent a critical corrective to the
contemporary dogma that mysticism is essentially monistic and
impersonal?

Hans Urs von Balthasar

The theological "aesthetics" and "theodrama" of the Swiss
theologian, Hans Urs von Balthasar, have much to say to those
Christians who prefer to emphasize the irreconcilable differences
between the Judeo-Christian religions and those of the East. In view
of this theologian's outstanding originality, creativity, depth, and
productivity, it is somewhat disappointing to find so few of his
German works available in English translation.[38]

Eastern religions highlight, for von Balthasar, what was once the common good of all peoples: religion as the distinguishing feature of what it means to be human. These religions dramatize, moreover, the human search and reaching-out from the world for the Absolute. The Judeo-Christian tradition, on the other hand, clearly illustrates *God's* initiative in seeking out the human, an initiative which reaches its high point in Jesus Christ, the invisible Father's only valid image.

The basic religious experience that the world of appearances, including our own empirical ego, cannot be the Absolute establishes the East's point of departure. If the experience of the chasm between the Absolute and our daily world is absolutized, then the world, the ego, etc., are declared "appearances," unreal, *maya*. The way of the East seeks the removal of all multiplicity through contact with the Absolute. By means of asceticism and methodical training, one may escape from the manifold, exterior world to the bliss of the One within. If this goal and technique are radicalized, then one seeks the dissolution of the ego and the world through an experience of undifferentiated unity in which only the Absolute remains.

Because God creates in order to communicate and reveal Himself, von Balthasar maintains that the search for God is written right into creation. Because of the basic human inclination toward the Absolute, God does not find indifference and unreceptivity when He reveals Himself. In a way similar to Merton's views on Zen and Zaehner's on enstatic yoga, von Balthasar considers Eastern religions to form the natural basis and the anthropological presuppositions for revealed religions. The Judeo-Christian religions, therefore, presuppose, preserve, and transform *natural* Eastern religions.

The Judeo-Christian tradition highlights God's personality and freedom, characteristics which von Balthasar sees obscured by to-day's philosophy and materialism, or replaced by meditation upon an impersonal Absolute. Everything, for von Balthasar, depends upon God's free initiative. The God of Moses, Abraham, and Jesus is the free Creator of the world which He affirmed as "very good," not as "appearance" or *maya*. God, moreover, establishes, affirms, and loves every created, free "I," an "I" firm enough from creation to allow the incarnation. Von Balthasar locates the special quality of Christian meditation in the experience of one's own and everyone else's individuality and uniqueness.

With respect to Western meditation techniques, von Balthasar notes that the Bible gives no specific instructions. Jesus taught his disciples not meditation exercises but simple vocal prayer. We know nothing, moreover, of Jesus' solitary prayer. Although Paul instructs Christians to pray always, the Christian tradition has never demanded from all the use of special techniques of prayer. Christianity has long recognized that "spiritual acrobatics" cannot compel God's grace. Can one who has mastered the various stages of yoga really be called "poor in spirit"? von Balthasar asks. True Christian conversion, on the other hand, comes from the divine initiative and not from techniques. The Christian meditates, moreover, to deepen his ability to recognize and to do God's will.

Both East and West, however, aim at destroying inner and outer attachments; cutting off the chains of passion; maintaining a distance from worldly attractions; mastering the tongue, the imagination, and distractions; concentrating the powers of soul; and securing true inner harmony and quiet.

With respect to meditation, however, East and West differ on two essential points. First of all, the practice of the love of neighbor in Eastern meditation is only a means or a preliminary stage to a higher vision. For example, Buddhist ethical selflessness, for von Balthasar, is only an aspect of metaphysical selflessness, for both "I" and "Thou" have no ultimate reality for the Buddhist. Genuine Christian love of neighbor, on the other hand, is always an end in itself. Even in the highest stages of mystical union, it never disappears.

Von Balthasar would therefore oppose Merton's view on Zen's alleged "love" and "personalism." To be sure, D.T. Suzuki, the Zen scholar who popularized it for the West, said that "the most important thing is love."[39] The Zen philosopher, Nishida, emphasized certain personal as well as transpersonal values. But if Buddhism really considers the self, the individual, to be *the* fundamental illusion, genuine love and personalism do not have any meaning when the other has no ultimate reality. For von Balthasar, incidental linguistic similarities may mask very different, and perhaps even irreconcilable, world views.

Secondly, like Zaehner, von Balthasar sees Eastern self-emptying techniques as attempting to reach a state of reflectionless *en*stasy, a being-in-oneself in perfect bliss. This Eastern "voiding" of consciousness is perhaps only an anthropological cleansing of the human spirit for a better vision of the divine light. With only superficial similarities to the Christian dark night of the soul which is a real participation in Christ's passion and death, it has no *special* Christian value for von Balthasar.

True Christian self-emptying, on the other hand, removes the barriers between God and the contemplative. It can involve an entire life of perfect, humble receptivity, a way of saying with one's entire being "Be it done to me according to thy will." It prepares, therefore, for the reception of God's word. This word is always both interior and, at the same time, an historically encountered human word. Christian interiority, moreover, must order the entire person by aiding a conversion to love. By bringing about a composed, integrated consciousness, it awakens the person to true sorrow, accepts and passes on the forgiveness received from God, and creates harmony between oneself and one's neighbor.

By concentrating the powers of the soul around its ground, both Eastern and Western mystical introversion, on the other hand, may result in a similar consciousness of undifferentiated unity. For von Balthasar, this experience is only the preliminary stage to true openness to God, the "standing on the peak" of R. C. Zaehner. It may be nothing more than the self-contemplation of the subject or a contemplation of the condition of possibility for conceptual consciousness. One may be contemplating a cosmic-enlarged consciousness, the God-image, or one's own desire for the Absolute. For von Balthasar, Underhill, and others, therefore, the question of what or whom the person is contemplating remains a serious question too easily short-circuited by the contemporary dogma that all mystical experience is essentially the same.

Detachment from self, for von Balthasar, is a common first step in both Eastern and Western meditation. The Buddhist moves away from the ego as a substantial center. The Christian detaches from the ego to be attached to God. For von Balthasar, the Christian experiences participation in a God beyond creation, but not removed from creation, a "boundless ultra-Thou" beyond objectification, but more intimate than the self. The Divine Center of the self bestows an experience of an ego both created and loved, which von Balthasar notes is the hallmark of Christian meditation. Furthermore, the

Christian experiences true mystical union with God, but not identity. Worship and adoration, not mystical identification or dissolution, characterize and guarantee this mystical union.

Because the highpoint of God's encounter with us occurs in Jesus Christ, von Balthasar stresses that God's historical self-revelation in Christ cannot be surpassed. Jesus Christ permeates all of salvation history, whether or not this is explicity adverted to in enstatic contemplation. Does the general Eastern disregard of history say anything significant about its spirituality and mysticism? Has Jesus' historical passion, death, and bodily resurrection, in addition to His own enlightenment, moreover, added a dimension to Christian mysticism insufficiently regarded by some who have turned East?

Von Balthasar's Christocentrism proceeds along two important lines. First of all, because of Jesus Christ, contemplation can neither be purely "transcendental" nor purely "categorical." Von Balthasar welds together in a most satisfying way the apophatic and kataphatic dimensions of Christian mysticism by his emphasis upon whoever sees Christ sees the Father. In short, genuine Christian contemplation for von Balthasar must always be *sacramental.* The *via affirmativa*—meditation upon concepts, images, and symbols—must lead out into an experience of the ever-greater God. The ways of forgetting and unknowing of the *via negativa* are not really denying whatever can be said of God, but underscoring the revealing and concealing fullness of the ever-greater God in the finite, sacramental reality.

Secondly, neither Buddhist compassion nor Eastern meditation as exoneration removes the incredible burden of worldly suffering. Only Golgotha takes away the sin and guilt of the world. There can be no Christian way to God, mystical or otherwise, which is not permeated by the Cross. Even St. Paul in the third heavens, bore the wounds of Christ and filled up what was lacking in Christ's sufferings. Jesus' high point, moreover, was his cry of abandonment on the Cross, not the light of Tabor. For von Balthasar, therefore, of highest value for the Christian is not the experience of transcendence, but the radical fidelity to the demands of daily life in faith, hope, and love. As the summit of human perfection, the counterpart to the Eastern yogin or Zen master is not the Christian mystic, but the Christian saint, whether or not she is a mystic.

Von Balthasar strongly criticizes the contemporary emphasis upon a technically learnable religious experience of God. He sees this as an attempt to subject religion to worldly science and to reduce it to a purely psychological affair. The implicit assumption that we should have worldly proof for all reality is a contemporary heresy found even within the Church. The quest for "experiences" haunts many today. The relationship of the person to God as Creator and the ground of all things is, however, never a question of direct experience.

Because the saints illustrate and exemplify new ways of imitating Christ in daily life, von Balthasar considers them a theological phenomenon and an important, neglected theme in theology. From the apostles to the Middle Ages, the great theologians were frequently saints. Life and teaching, orthopraxis and orthodoxy mutually fructified, nourished, and supported each other.

For von Balthasar, the most important thing about the saints is not their heroic, personal accomplishments, but their firm obedience and total commitment to their *mission.* He emphasizes time and again the stance of the saints in quiet concentration and attentiveness: "Speak, Lord, your servant hears." Total availability is the genuine Christian analogue to Eastern meditative selflessness. The saints experience a great commissioning and are dismissed from God to the world and to their fellow men. Here can be found Christianity's powerful worldly orientation.

Von Balthasar has also creatively displaced the alleged dualism between prayer and deed, contemplation and action. The Christian who accepts the good news experiences the love of God which has conquered the world, wants to know only Christ crucified, and goes to the Source of all as a child goes to its Father. To rest mystically in the Source of all, however, is to participate in an eternal Love which has proven itself precisely as Love in its exertion for the world. The Source of Grace from which the mystic drinks is already God's absolute action for the world.

The Christian mystic experiences, therefore, a Godhead turned toward action in the incarnation, cross and resurrection. It is impossible to get behind the God who has loved, died, and risen for us to contemplate an eternal, primordial divine essence in eternal rest in itself. To contemplate God's Love is to be involved in God's activity for the world in Christ crucified. And to be involved in God's action, we must love others, because we have been loved first through God's praxis. Moreover, to proceed correctly in praxis, according to von Balthasar, is at the same time to contemplate more deeply the Source of all. This dialectic must never be simplified nor eliminated. The Johannine word "remain" says it all: to "remain" in a Love which is God and God's action for the world.

Some would contend, however, that von Balthasar's approach (like Teilhard's) suffers from its too hasty assessment and insufficiently nuanced use of the term "Eastern meditation." Because of God's universal Self-communication, some would also question von Balthasar's position that one finds outside of the Judeo-Christian tradition only "natural" religions.

Can Eastern meditation, moreover, really be reduced to a "technique"? Are spiritual pride and the reliance upon human effort only the domain of the East? Does the Judeo-Christian tradition have a monopoly upon humble receptivity, sensitivity to God's will, and a sense of mission? Is not William Johnston perhaps closer to the truth when he shows the great similarities between the "nothingness" of the Christian apophatic tradition and Buddhist "nothingness," between Buddhist self-emptying and Christian *kenosis*? On the other hand, von Balthasar and Teilhard both see eye-to-eye in underscoring Christianity's strong personalistic basis, i.e., the value of each human "I" before the personal God of love, and the lack of personalism which permeates much of Eastern religions.

What von Balthasar says about the Christian saints should also be said about the non-Christian saints: they are very important sources for a contemporary Christian theology. Some Christian theologians maintain that the "turn East" must be one essential aspect of all contemporary Christian theology, spirituality, and mysticism.

Some commentators would de-emphasize the somewhat outdated German stress on Christ's "abandonment by God" on the Cross to re-emphasize Christ's bodily resurrection. Finally, even some writers, like Johnston, who would agree with von Balthasar in distinguishing East from West, still prefer to pay more attention to the fruits of the great variety of mystical experiences for daily living. Where self-control, faithfulness, love, joy, kindness, goodness, peace, patience, and gentleness reign—be it East or West—there is the Spirit of God.

Harvey Cox

From a perspective much different from Teilhard's and von Balthasar's, Harvey Cox has called attention to an unprecedented American phenomenon.[40] Without actually going East, thousands of Americans have "turned East" by dropping the traditional Judeo-Christian religions to practice Eastern religions in varying degrees of seriousness.

White, educated, middle and upper-middle class, and usually having had some university and drug experience, these Eastern-turners are searching for deep friendships in new forms of community. They desire richer and more immediate experiences of life. They want practice and not merely assent to dogmas of faith. They also seem to hunger for a stable form of authority, the all-knowing teacher. For some, the East's alleged simplicity fits in with contemporary interest in health and ecology. Still others look to the East for a solution to the male-dominated faiths of the West.

Cox notes a certain irony in all of this. At a time when so many Americans are falling in love with a mythical East which perhaps never existed, Asians are turning to the West for science, technology, and even for political and cultural forms. The very same forces, therefore, which brought about disillusionment with the biblical faiths are rapidly penetrating the East.

For Cox, turning East is for the most part an illusory "turning-back" in search of original innocence. Turning East will not solve the problems of contemporary life. In fact, the comfort it offers is, at most, short-term. The quest for instant security and freedom from depression and the illusion that God is found only in "peak experiences" turn neo-Orientalism into an anodyne which eliminates a whole range of human experience. Cox stresses that in any authentic mystical tradition genuine enlightenment and peace come only through radical purification.

He has also discovered that most American versions of Oriental religions have only a superficial similarity to their classical Eastern counterparts. Many offer a simplified blending of Eastern meditation techniques, Eastern mystical jargon, the occult, Christian images, and Western patterns of organization. Gimmickry, faddism, spiritual oneupmanship, phoniness, and the promise of cheap comfort predominate.[41]

Cox further contends that Western psychology has turned to the East to save itself from its own inner bankruptcy. The psychologizing of the East, however, essentially emasculates these great religions of their saving power. They are reduced to mental health gimmicks pandering to the West's preoccupation with self. Neo-Orientalism promotes a new gluttony, the hunger for all experience, radical narcissism, a new consumerism of the spirit. It has become one more consumer product in a society in transition from material to spiritual gluttony.

Christianity preaches love, self-sacrifice, and the Cross. Buddhism preaches compassion, detachment, the non-self, and the unity of all things. The biblical God of grace, moreover, is full of surprises and frequently plays "havoc with social roles" (p. 80). Buddhism stresses egolessness and emptiness. Both have nothing in common with the American interest in narcissistic self-improvement. As Cox says: "Neither in Buddhism nor in Christianity is meditation a method for self-discovery or self-actualization" (p. 77).

Cox has also found many Eastern-turners to be drifters without roots or fidelity to anything or anyone. Their pseudo-Buddhism dangerously combines a "loveless ego with psychological 'detachment' " (p. 140). In fact, their irresponsibility, their inability for deep commitments, their misuse and discarding of people for their selfish whims masquerade as Buddhist detachment. This "throw-away" detachment undermines genuine Buddhism, for Cox. As Carl Jung pointed out years ago, Cox maintains that few Westerners can genuinely turn East.

Summary

This section has presented a vigorous repudiation of some of the views seen in previous sections. The way of the East, for Teilhard and von Balthasar, is essentially the human effort for God. These religions, however, extinguish love, personalism, and action because of their insistence upon dissolution in an impersonal Absolute. The Judeo-Christian tradition involves God's free and personal turning toward humanity. It preaches a personal God who loves and affirms what He has created, especially the finite "I." Both Teilhard and von Balthasar consider the Western emphasis upon a love union of differentiated unity far superior to the East's undifferentiated union with an impersonal Absolute.

For Teilhard, only Christianity can synthesize the human mystical desire for personal union with God, other persons, and the world. Moreover, only Christianity takes evolution and time seriously. Teilhard rejected, therefore, the "common core" view of Huxley and others which attempted to reduce all religions to certain common factors. He favored a new synthesis, a Christianity extended beyond itself, one which loved evolution, the world, and God.

The mysticisms of Teilhard and von Balthasar are highly Christocentric. For Teilhard, evolution is becoming the cosmic Christ. All human action toward building a better world and all human suffering accepted only after fully fighting against evil go into experiencing and "building" the cosmic Christ.

For von Balthasar, because the visible Christ is the valid image of the invisible Father, all genuine contemplation must be sacramental. He sees Eastern contemplation almost exclusively in terms of human effort, techniques, and enstasy; Christianity, however, he sees in terms of grace, calling, heroic charity, service to the world, and openness to God's will. He pointedly calls attention to the value of the saints as theological sources. Because God is the One who suffered, died, and rose for the world, von Balthasar views all genuine contemplation as action and vice versa. Finally, Cox has stressed the spiritual gluttony and narcissism infecting so much of America's neo-Orientalism.

With Ursula King, however, the question can be asked: Have Teilhard and von Balthasar accurately and fairly represented Eastern religions?

This provides a good transition point to the next section dealing with the new mystical theology of one very important theologian, Karl Rahner, S.J.

8
A Contemporary Mystical Theology

Karl Rahner

Karl Rahner is one of the few theologians of this century to give serious consideration to the mystics and their writings as valuable theological sources. The mystics do theology, for Rahner, because they teach "something about mysticism."[1] The *Spiritual Exercises,* and other mystical classics, for example, are important because they are a "creative prototype . . . [and] a subject of tomorrow's theology."[2] The great mystics, moreover, present a paradigm, a clarification, and an illumination of what takes place everywhere in faith, hope, and love. We see more clearly and explicitly in their lives what is taking place in the lives of all persons of good faith. Rahner stands, therefore, as a critical corrective both to the Continental Protestant tendency to dismiss mysticism as heresy and to the traditional Catholic isolation of mysticism from the other areas of theology. These are only a few reasons why Rahner has chided his fellow theologians for their lack of interest in mystical questions.

The mystics, moreover, illustrate what contemporary theology should be doing and what Rahner's "mystagogical" theology is, in fact, doing: initiating us into the experience of Mystery, Revelation, and Love which haunts the roots of our being and has incarnated itself in the life, death, and resurrection of Jesus Christ. The essential task of today's Christian theology as a whole and of Christian mystical theology in particular, for Rahner, is to make intelligible that our basic mystical experience of being referred to Mystery is already present in the simplest acts of faith, hope, and love which permeate daily life.

Christian theology must also reflect upon the indissoluble difference between the primordial experience of our reference to God and the interpretations given this experience. Interpretations may be true or false, adequate or inadequate. For Rahner, moreover, a genuine mysticism may coexist with an insufficient mystical philosophy or theology, with truncated interpretations of this original mystical experience found in every human heart. On the other hand, whether contradictions between various mystical philosophies and theologies result from different horizons of interpretation of one primordial mystical experience or from actually different mystical experiences is, for Rahner, a key question in today's mystical dialogue between East and West.

Although Rahner places much emphasis upon the difference between experience and interpretation, he notes that Christianity has never considered interpretation unimportant, superfluous, or even extrinsic. Experience and interpretation form a mutually conditioning unity. False interpretations may change or even destroy the primordial mystical experience. Theory, for Rahner, may become a person's lived orientation.

Because of God's universal salvific will and radical *Self*-communication to all persons, *everyone* is called to the immediacy of God's presence, a call which, of course, can be rejected. A supernatural, graced, "anonymously Christian" mysticism may, according to Rahner, exist outside of an explicit Christianity. He writes:

> In every human being . . . there is something like an anonymous, unthematic, perhaps repressed, basic experience of being orientated to God, which is constitutive of man in his concrete make-up (of nature and grace), which can be repressed but not destroyed, which is "mystical" or (if you prefer a more cautious terminology) has its climax in what the older teachers called infused contemplation.[3]

Man is, therefore, mystical man, experientially referred to a holy, loving Mystery. Even non-Christian religions, for Rahner, may contain and nurture a graced mysticism. Even if the mystical experience of one's reference to the God of love is not interpreted in Christian terms, Rahner maintains that this does not necessarily mean that we are dealing with "natural," "pagan," or "demonic" mysticisms.

In classical fashion, Rahner defines mysticism as "infused contemplation, in which God gratuitously makes himself known to the individual."[4] On the other hand, the religious experiences of the saints supply him with "a vague empirical concept of Christian mysticism."[5] He writes:

> ... all that they experienced of closeness to God, of higher impulses, of visions, inspirations, of the consciousness of being under the special and personal guidance of the Holy Spirit, of ecstasies, etc., all this is comprised in our understanding of the word mysticism, without our having to stop here to ask ... in what more precisely this proper element consists.[6]

The extraordinary mystical experiences of the saints, however, never surpass supernatural faith, hope, and love. Between the beatific vision and the everyday life of Christian faith, hope, and love, no intermediary stage exists. Theologically speaking, for Rahner, "mystical experience is not specifically different from the ordinary life of grace (as such)."[7]

Rahner places the difference between the saints' unusual experiences (mysticism in the strict sense) and ordinary Christian experiences (mysticism in a wide sense) in the person's natural domain. The saints experienced in an extraordinarily psychological way what all Christians experience in a more hidden way. *Psychologically* speaking, Rahner distinguishes mystical experiences in the strict sense from those in the wide sense insofar as the former's natural, psychological foundation differs from those found in daily life. The specific way in which the saints deepen, purify, and radicalize the normal life of faith belongs to *natural* psychology and to the person's *natural* ability for concentration, meditation, enstasy, self-emptying, and other contemplative techniques usually associated with Eastern religions.

The "unusual psychological manifestation" is a "natural, pure experience of transcendence when the mediation of categories either partly or completely ceases."[8] For Rahner, mysticism in the strict sense involves a "purely nonconceptual experience of transcendence without imagery."[9] When a person's graced orientation to God emerges explicitly into awareness to occupy the person's center of consciousness without the usual mediation of images and concepts, this is mysticism in the strict sense. When all is placed in the cloud of forgetting, as taught in *The Cloud of Unknowing,* consciousness is full of a love for God beyond images, concepts, and ideas. The natural component here, however, is the person's presence-to-self whenever she is present to anything else, the natural ability to "return-to-self" when present to another. During this "return-to-self," the usually only implicit experience of our orientation to God becomes more explicit and dominates consciousness in a way only vaguely experienced in normal consciousness.

To be sure, Rahner does argue for a "difference in kind" between transcendence (orientation to God) "as the necessary condition of any act of the mind, even the most ordinary, and transcendence explicitly experienced."[10] When our ever-present, implicit experience of being referred to God occupies the center stage of our consciousness, there is a qualitative difference. For terminological reasons, therefore, Rahner would reserve the word "mysticism" for only these unusually pure and intense psychological experiences of our graced orientation to the God of love. The difference, however, between the mysticism of the saints and the less explicit form of ordinary Christian life is not a supernatural difference. The difference belongs to "the natural order of psychology and parapsychology."[11]

Because the essence of Christian mysticism involves an implicit or an explicit experience of our graced orientation to God, Rahner maintains that there is no purely "natural mysticism." On the other hand, he calls attention to psychologically unusual experiences which do not involve our graced orientation to God, but still seem to be "mystical" in some sense. By means of psychological training, for example, a person may achieve an extremely intense and clear experience of bodiliness, of enstasy, of the voiding of consciousness, of biological-psychological dispositions, of the unconscious, of the depth consciousness, of collective archetypes, of the "id," etc.

Psycho-technical training can produce these experiences even in a non-religious context. Because they are not necessarily linked with the person's graced orientation to God and can take place outside of the sphere of moral decisions, Rahner calls them *actus indifferentes* (morally neutral acts). He cautiously suggests that they be called "parapsychological phenomena," not mystical phenomena.

Because these parapsychological phenomena frequently occur with genuine religious mystical experience, he labels them "mystical," at least in the broad sense. As "assisting graces," moreover, they can prepare the person for a more explicit awareness of the reference to the God of love. They may also anchor the acts of faith, hope, and love more deeply in the person. And just as Christianity makes use of secular psychology to nurture genuine faith, hope, and love, so, too, should Christianity make its own the psychosomatic "technology" available from Eastern religions.

Within this context, Rahner discusses charismatic phenomena which he calls "mysticism in ordinary dress" and "the mysticism of the masses."[12] Speaking in tongues, dramatic faith conversions, faith healings, prophecy, etc., are neither pure experiences of the Holy Spirit nor nonsense having no significance for Christian living and salvation. They seem to be psychological or parapsychological phenomena which arise from the person's natural psychological structure for religious and non-religious reasons. Secular psychology can and should study these phenomena. If genuinely religious, these experiences bring more explicitly into consciousness the person's primordial experience of God.

They could be the reverberations, the echoes from the person's mystical center, overflowing into and actuating the various dimensions and levels of the person's psychic structure. Genuine charismatic phenomena may blend, therefore, an experience of the Holy Spirit with unusual psychic phenomena. These experiences may express both the presence of the Holy Spirit and the person's psychological structure. They may be the psychosomatic result of a deep experience of grace. Or they may be an unusual psychological experience which brings the person's experience of graced orientation to God more clearly to the fore by anchoring the basic act of faith, hope, and love more deeply.

By distinguishing mystical experiences as those which belong intrinsically to our graced reference to God from parapsychological phenomena which do not, Rahner stresses that in the practical course of life, all genuine experiences of transcendence are *graced*. For him, therefore, there is no "natural" mysticism. His position, however, is painfully nuanced, for as he asks:

> But the question then arises as to whether mysticism out-side Christianity (which certainly exists) is an "anony-mously" Christian and therefore grace-inspired mysticism. Or, on the other hand, is Christian mysticism a "natural" mysticism just like non-Christian, although obviously un-der the influence of grace like all other free moral actions of a human being, purified and free from baser elements like all that is naturally moral? Or are these two questions aimed after all at the same thing?[13]

Rahner seems to be saying that, *theologically* speaking, all mysticism, even outside of Christianity, is graced, because all mysti-cism involves the experience of our primordial, graced orientation to the God of love. *Psychologically* speaking, however, all mysticism is natural, even Christian mysticism, because all mysticism involves the natural "self-presence," or "return-to-self," concomitant in every act of knowledge and love.

For Rahner, some mystical experiences may be the experience of one's own pure spirituality, a graced spirituality, but not necessari-ly experienced as such. Rahner seems to mean this when he writes of "at least one awareness which is not consciousness of an *object:* the concomitant self-awareness of every act of the mind."[14] He definitely means this when he describes a mysticism which "is simply the person's experience of his own pure spirituality."[15]

On the basis of Rahner's theological anthropology and of phe-nomenological descriptions of some mystical experiences, there seem to be mystical experiences of the self with no *explicit* reference to God. To be sure, for Rahner, any authentic experience of the self is an authentic experience of God.[16] The experiential reference to God in any genuine experience of self, however, may remain hidden, anonymous, or even repressed, for a whole variety of reasons.

Finally, Rahner's position seems to allow for a mysticism of our transcendental relationship to this world as "spirit-in-world." He has

expressly cautioned against confusing an experience of oneness with
the world with the experience of God. Furthermore, Rahner has
argued that at death the human soul becomes "pancosmic" and not
"acosmic," i.e.,

> enters into a much closer, more intimate relationship to
> that ground of the unity of the universe which is hard to
> conceive yet is very real, and in which all things in the
> world are interrelated and communicate anteriorly to any
> mutual influence upon each other.[17]

Could not "cosmic consciousness," mystical experiences of "nature,"
and perhaps even Zen *satori* experiences be earthly foreshadowings
of the pancosmic experience at death? Are there not mystical experiences in this life which underscore the spirit-*in-world* aspect of
human existence?

Against those who would deny the value of a systematically and
technically developed mysticism, Rahner maintains that it can be a
valid and significant way to Christian perfection. On the other hand,
he rejects the elitist interpretation that only trained mystics can reach
Christian perfection. Mystical experience, according to Rahner, may
take place outside of psychotechnical effort and is definitely not
limited to a selected few. Fidelity to daily life in faith, hope, and love
provides the basis for his "mysticism of everyday life."

For example, the experience of utter loneliness; forgiveness
without expectation of being rewarded or even of feeling good about
one's selflessness; radical fidelity to the depths of one's conscience,
even when one appears like a fool before others; faithfulness, hope,
and love, even when there are no apparent reasons for so acting; the
bitter experience of the wide gulf between what we truly desire and
what life actually gives us; a silent hope in the face of death—these
and similar experiences are the experiences of the mysticism of daily
life.

Even the atheist who lives moderately, selflessly, honestly, cou-
rageously, and who silently serves others experiences the mysticism
of everyday life. Perhaps *the* secular mystical experience is the
courageous, total acceptance of life and of oneself when everything
tangible seems to be collapsing. Anyone who does this has implicitly

accepted the holy Mystery which fills the emptiness of both life and oneself.

Because of the unity of the love of God and neighbor, perhaps the most contemporary form of the mysticism of everyday life is the unreserved love for another.[18] Genuine love of neighbor is truly mystical. As Rahner writes:

> It must be realized that in earthly man this emptying of self will not be accomplished by practicing pure inwardness, but by real activity which is called humility, service, love of our neighbor, the cross and death. One must descend into hell together with Christ; lose one's soul, not directly to the God who is above all names but in the service of one's brethren.[19]

From the above, it seems clear that Rahner's approach to mysticism is hardly that of pure inwardness and interiority. In fact, along with Ignatius, he stresses a finding of God in all things, a mysticism of joy in the world, and an Easter faith which loves the earth. A loving, transforming Mystery has created all things, communicated Himself to all things, and embraces all things—even the most humble aspects of daily living. There can be, therefore, a mysticism of everyday things: of work, of sleep, of eating, of drinking, of seeing, of sitting, and of standing.[20]

Rahner defines mysticism as "the radical experience of faith which destroys the conceptual and the categorial in so far as these claim to be ultimate realities."[21] This echoes the admonition of *The Cloud of Unknowing* to place all created things in a cloud of forgetting so that a cloud of unknowing may arise between God and the contemplative. Only naked love may pierce the cloud of unknowing. If genuine mysticism means dying to all created things to surrender totally to loving Mystery, the death and resurrection of Jesus Christ is the paradigm of perfect mysticism. Christ is the perfect, enfleshed, mystical Word. His death remains paradigmatic for the perfect detachment from all created things required for perfect surrender to Mystery. His bodily resurrection is the paradigm of Mystery's acceptance and confirmation of total self-surrender, that dying to self and to all created things is not ultimately absurd.

All mysticism, therefore, has an objective relationship to Jesus Christ, according to Rahner. Non-Christian religions and much of the mysticism of daily life, of course, do not explicitly grasp this. To detach oneself from oneself and from all created things to surrender lovingly, albeit often anonymously, to the ultimate Mystery of life requires participation in the death of Christ. To experience such dying as not in vain is to participate in his resurrection. Just as Christ understood love for the least of his brethren as love for him (even from those who did not know him), so can all genuine mysticism be interpreted as a "seeking Christology." The death and resurrection of Jesus Christ present the historical visibility and tangibility of mysticism's origin, dynamism, goal, success, and final transformation.

Another very important point in Rahner's mystical theology centers on the notion of created intermediaries with respect to the person's mystical relationship with God. The historical reality of Christ, the Church, the sacraments, the preached word, etc., constitute intrinsic elements of the person's primordial orientation to God. Created realities need not disappear for God to be experienced. Rahner's incarnational stance insists that creaturely mediation does not destroy or remove the immediate relationship of the graced person to God. In fact, it makes it possible, guarantees it, and attests to it in the historical-categorical dimensions of human life. The incarnation demonstrates that creatures are not mere "representations" of an ever-distant God. God is here with us and can be found in all things. If and insofar as Eastern mysticisms deny mediation, then the human person must disappear in a mystical theophany, destroying the significance of history and creation. This is, of course, unchristian and unacceptable.

Rahner's mystical theology creatively synthesizes the best elements of mysticism with and without images, signs, and symbols, i.e., the kataphatic and apophatic mystical traditions. He writes:

> . . . this basic incarnational structure of the unconfused unity of God and his creatures gives us to understand that we can apprehend God in the sign (or in the form of a vision) only if we do not cling to the sign . . . as if it were the ultimate reality, God himself. The sign must be welcomed and passed by, grasped and relinquished.[22]

The kataphatic tradition—the way of images, signs, and symbols—as found in St. Teresa of Avila, St. Ignatius of Loyola, St. Catherine of Siena, etc., is more in keeping with Christianity's historical, incarnational character. The apophatic tradition—the way of silent, imageless mysticism—as found in *The Cloud of Unknowing*, St. John of the Cross, etc., highlights the ever-greater God beyond all representation. Still, as Rahner says, God will "one day reveal himself even to the pure mystic as the God of the transfigured earth because he is more than pure spirit."[23]

For Rahner, therefore, there can be no purely apophatic nor kataphatic mysticism, even outside of Christianity. Insofar as Christian mysticism is *Christian,* there must be kataphatic, incarnational elements. Insofar as Christian mysticism is *mysticism,* there must be apophatic elements which bring the person into the presence of the ever-greater God. For Rahner, moreover, the incarnational image, symbol, and representation become transparent to lead the person into God's Mystery. Is this not the "sacramental contemplation" of von Balthasar which so strongly opposes the undifferentiated unity emphasis of Stace and others?

Summary

Rahner, like von Balthasar, has creatively turned to the mystics and saints as theological sources. By rethinking Christian theology in the light of mystical experience, he has gone a long way in meeting one of Johnston's demands. With Underhill, he finds in the mystics a paradigm of the life of genuine faith, hope, and love.

One aspect of Rahner's theology is to evoke, deepen, and make more explicit *every* person's core experience of reference to a holy, loving Mystery. Another aspect is the unfolding of the Christian mysteries of salvation history which recognizes their root unity in God's Mystery as Self-communication to all persons. Both Rahner and von Balthasar agree on the importance of salvation history.

For Rahner, no mysticism is purely "natural." He also speaks of graced non-Christian mysticisms. Both of these points put him at odds with von Balthasar, Zaehner, Teilhard, perhaps Merton, and those commentators who refuse to speak about grace under any circumstance. Like Zaehner, however, he does distinguish between an experience of God, of self, and of the world. On the other hand, these experiences are always grace-supported, although their specific graced quality may remain only implicit.

For Rahner, mysticism is essentially the non-conceptual, graced experience of our basic orientation to God which occurs non-conceptually in the return-to-self concomitant in every act of knowledge and love. Like Stace, he sharply distinguishes experience and interpretation. With Johnston and perhaps Katz, however, he sees interpretation as important and intrinsic to experience itself.

The unusual experiences of the saints differ from the faith, hope, and love experiences of "ordinary" Christians only in the realm of psychology. Rahner further distinguishes the mystical experience of our graced orientation to Mystery from parapsychological experiences. Like Merton's "masked contemplation," Rahner argues for a "mysticism of everyday life," hidden experiences of self-surrender to Mystery which may occur in all walks of life and under any circumstances. Similar to Teilhard and von Balthasar, Rahner contends that all genuine mysticism is Christocentric.

His ability to link extraordinary Christian mysticism, the mysticism of everyday life, non-Christian mysticisms, secular mysticism, love of neighbor, charismatic and parapsychological phenomena to a common root, but not to a common denominator, makes him truly the "Father of the Church of the twentieth century" and the "mystical doctor" of our age.

9
A Future Mystical Theology

Bernard Lonergan

Bernard Lonergan, S.J. stands as one of the most significant thinkers and theologians of the twentieth century. His works can provide the solid foundation necessary for the successful transposition of traditional mystical theology into a much needed contemporary framework for three reasons.

First of all, by correlating the basic insights of St. Thomas Aquinas with contemporary physics and mathematics, he has disclosed what theology and the secular sciences have in common: fidelity to the basic dynamism of the mind to be attentive, intelligent, reasonable, and responsible. Both theology and science, therefore, have a mystical basis. Their very dynamics, for Lonergan, raise the question of ultimate truth, value, and authenticity. His strongly empirical bent and interdisciplinary emphasis, moreover, prod a yet-to-be interdisciplinary mystical-theology team to assimilate the results of the various contemporary sciences for what Johnston has called "the new science of mysticism."

Second, Lonergan has pinpointed the desire of faith to surrender itself in unrestricted love as the transcultural dimension of the world's great religions. Rejecting the classicist's claim of only one authentic culture, Lonergan argues for many cultures. As Johnston has noted, Lonergan's transcendental precepts of being attentive, intelligent, reasonable, responsible, and in love remain invariant through cultural change and differences. In any given culture, who is

the authentic person? Whoever is attentive, intelligent, reasonable, responsible, and has surrendered to the demands of unrestricted love. The basic mystical dynamism of the human spirit can provide, therefore, the basis for ecumenical dialogue among the world's great religions.

So, too, by distinguishing faith from its formulations in beliefs, Lonergan stresses the transcultural, other-worldly mystical dimension of all authentic cultures. God's gift of love is the transcultural inner core of authentic religion which manifests itself in a variety of ways. This transcultural, mystical dimension, a self-fulfillment in holiness from God's gift of love, provides the common basis for dialogue between Christians, non-Christians, and even atheists.

Third, because Lonergan conceives theology primarily as a method, i.e., "a normative pattern of recurrent and related operations yielding cumulative and progressive results" (p. 4),[1] he speaks to many who consider method to be the key to future interdisciplinary work. Mystical theology in an age of science, technology, relativity, statistical analysis, psychoanalysis, biofeedback, psychedelic drugs, philosophical and theological pluralism, ecumenics, and the East-West dialogue can find in Lonergan's theological method based on the inherently mystical dynamism of the mind one of the best ways to correlate critically and comprehensively religion, science, and culture.

According to Lonergan, religion as total commitment supplies the raw material for theology. Theology in turn performs a mediating function between a culture and the meaning and value of religion in that culture. Theology must reflect upon a religion and focus upon the interdependence, the mutual relationships, and the correlations between a religion and its cultural matrix.

Theology comprises two basic phases, a mediat*ing* and a mediat*ed* phase. In the first phase, one must listen to the divine word, carefully read the relevant texts, and make the tradition one's own through as radical an encounter with the past as possible. "In brief," Lonergan writes, "there is a theology *in oratione obliqua* [in indirect discourse] that tells what Paul and John, Augustine and Aquinas, and anyone else had to say about God and the economy of salvation" (p. 133). This first phase is mediat*ing* theology.

This listening and mediating theology consists of four functional specialties: research, interpretation, history, and dialectic. Research turns to a religion's sources to collect and to make the data available. Interpretation focuses upon what the data means, how one is to understand this data. History seeks out the ongoing movements, the flow, to narrate and to judge what has taken place. Dialectic looks at the push-and-pull, the sources of conflicts in history, interpretation, and research. It takes different points of view seriously, seeks to eliminate merely apparent differences, and aims ultimately at a comprehensive viewpoint.

Theology's second phase bears witness to the word, raises critical questions about what has been read, discovers the responsibility it has to pass on the tradition intact, and takes a position with respect to the future. This speaking phase is media*ted* theology, "a theology *in oratione recta* [in direct discourse] in which the theologian, enlightened by the past, confronts the problems of his own day" (p. 133).

Mediated theology also consists of four functional specialties: foundations, doctrines, systematics, and communications. Foundations explicates and objectifies the human authenticity resulting from intellectual, moral, and religious conversion. It explicitly thematizes conversion by objectifying the intrinsic transformation of the subject and her world. Foundations brings to explicit consciousness what is implicit in the exercise of vertical liberty, that liberty which selects one's basic stance toward reality. As Lonergan says, "a vertical exercise is the set of judgments and decisions by which we move from one horizon to another" (p. 237), usually to one more comprehensive. Foundations takes place on the fourth level of consciousness, the level of decision. One decides here who and what one wishes to be. This decision about one's world-view provides the needed foundation which moves the person from the first phase of theology "that sets forth the convictions and opinions of others to the direct discourse that states what is so" (p. 267).

Doctrines explicate the doctrinal edifice which flows from conversion, i.e., the teachings associated with the decision of faith. Systematics aims at understanding the realities affirmed in doctrines; it orders and systematizes them to provide a holistic vision. Communications seeks the manifold ways the intelligible riches of a religion can be imparted to a given culture at any particular time.

Lonergan's functional specialities also arise because of the four levels of consciousness and intentionality. Intentionality makes objects present to us; consciousness makes us present to ourselves. To be authentically human, the human mind should move from experiencing, to understanding, to judging, and finally to deciding. We should be attentive to be intelligent, to understand; be intelligent to be reasonable, to judge; and be reasonable to be responsible, to decide. Attention and wonder find their fulfillment in insight; insight finds its fulfillment in truth and verification. Truth and verification find their fulfillment in embracing the real and doing the good.

According to the four levels of consciousness and intentionality in normal sequence, Lonergan correlates research with the level of experiencing, interpretation with understanding, history with judgment, and dialectic with decision. In inverse sequence, foundations is correlated with the level of decision, doctrines with judgment, systematics with understanding, and communications with experiencing. To be sure, the theologian whose work is a particular functional specialty operates on all four levels of consciousness and intentionality. His goal, however, is the end proper to that level of consciousness and intentionality corresponding to his functional specialty.

The four interlocking and interrelated stages and levels of consciousness find fulfillment in authenticity, in being religious, in being in love with God. Attentive experience, intelligent understanding, and well-balanced judgment should culminate in rational love. The perfection of consciousness, for Lonergan, consists in realistic love. By radically asking what the data means, by demanding to know if the mind's explanatory insights are correct, true, real, and what value they have is to attain intellectual, rational, and moral self-transcendence. The very dynamism of the human mind, frequently catalyzed by its encounter with evil and negativity, contains the question of ultimate intelligence, reason, and value. If, for Lonergan, the question of God is intrinsic to all questioning, "being in love with God is the basic fulfillment of our conscious intentionality" (p. 105).

Although Lonergan distinguishes being religious from doing theology, he refuses to separate them. Religious conversion is not only required for moving from the first to the second phase of theology; it also plays a primary role in the first phase. Religious conversion radically transforms the theologian. "Conversion, as

lived," writes Lonergan, "affects all of man's conscious and inten-
tional operations. It directs his gaze, pervades his imagination, releases the symbols that penetrate to the depths of his psyche" (p.
131).[2] He provides, therefore, a strong counterpoint to those many
contemporary theologians who tend to divorce the theologian's living sprituality from his theological "objectivity."

Conversion transforms the person, bestows a new set of roots,
and alters her stance toward reality. The person who falls in love
with God without restrictions or reservations experiences a collapse
of her previous horizon for knowing, choosing, deciding, and doing.
Loving God with one's whole heart, mind, strength, and soul "sets
up a new horizon in which the love of God will transform our
knowing" (p. 106). When God's gift of love takes over the core of a
person's being, it becomes the efficacious ground for all self-transcendence. It changes how a person seeks truth, realizes values, and
stands vis-à-vis the universe, its ground, and its goal.

This other-worldly falling in love with God gives rise to faith, to
loving-knowledge. "Faith is the knowledge born of religious love" (p.
115), for Lonergan. If, in the usual course of events, knowledge
precedes love, in religious matters love precedes knowledge. And it is
truly a faith-knowledge, a loving-knowledge, which results from
God's love flooding our innermost being. Faith as the eye of religious
love is "the knowledge reached through the discernment of values
and the judgment of value of a person in love" (p. 115). If the heart
has its reasons which the mind does not know, these reasons are the
reasons of faith.

The experience of the mystery of God's love usually "remains
within subjectivity as a vector, an undertow, a fateful call to a
dreaded holiness" (p. 113). Being in love is a fact which makes the
individual what he is. It may speak with a loud or a soft voice in any
given individual. For the mystic, this voice is so loud that he
withdraws "from the world mediated by meaning into a silent and
all-absorbing self-surrender in response to God's gift of love" (p.
273). Lonergan sees this as mysticism's "main component," although
he points out the great variety of ways in which mysticism may be
attained and express itself. Frequently, however, because the mystic
is so explicitly aware of being in love with God, her religiously
differentiated consciousness prefers the negations of an apophatic

theology. This highlights the fact that there are *no* qualifications or conditions on this love.

Be that as it may, the experience of being in love with God varies from person to person and also during the lifetime of any given person. It provides, however, the silent or the loud ambience, the atmosphere, the weak or powerful urgings and goadings to the theological enterprise. To be in love with God is no longer to be one's own. It is not an achievement, but God's free gift of Himself. It establishes the first principle of one's being, enabling one to grasp both conclusions and principles. For Lonergan, it is an unassailable fact, for "if one is deceiving oneself one is not in love . . . love proves itself."[3]

Unrestricted, unconditional love of God differs as defined and as achieved. As defined, "it is the habitual actuation of man's capacity for self-transcendence" (p. 283). As religious conversion, it provides the basis for moral and intellectual conversion. As experienced in oneself or found in others, one realizes that it is self-verifying and the one norm against which everything else is to be measured. Authenticity is self-validating, therefore, despite its never-total victory over the unauthentic in the life of any given person. Even the saints must confess their sins.

Lonergan has developed a theology rooted in honesty and love, flowing from a self grasped by God's unconditional love, and a self structured by judgment and decision. Through surrender to the transcendental precepts, the basic dynamisms of the human spirit to be attentive, be intelligent, be reasonable, be responsible, and be in love, human authenticity arises. Neither principles of logic nor extrinsic, moralistic slogans, the transcendental precepts are the very life and power of the human spirit, "the native spontaneities and inevitabilities of our consciousness" (p. 18). To surrender to the basic demands of the human spirit is to move from unauthenticity to authenticity; it is to experience intellectual, moral, and religious conversion. To renege on the proddings of the transcendental precepts is to suffer intellectual, moral, and religious blindness and aberration; it is to become unauthentic, unfulfilled, and less human.

With a theology and the sciences solidly rooted in the authenticity of the human subject, Lonergan is able to redintegrate Eastern and Western mysticisms, science, and academic theology. Because the subject in love must love all that God loves, hence, the world, Lonergan provides the point of contact for mysticism and political theology. Holiness, human skills, and human affairs are inextricably bound together. For Lonergan, moreover, "faith is linked with human progress and it has to meet the challenge of human decline" (p. 117).[4]

The field of mystical theology awaits theologians to transpose the old mystical theology into a new mystical theology based on Lonergan's eight functional specialities. Has an adequate and contemporary mystical dialectic been established? How adequate are the existing histories of mysticism? Interpretation and research, too, must be transposed. This age also calls for a new foundation for mystical theology, a new set of doctrines which flows from this foundation, a contemporary systematization of these doctrines, and, finally, their effective communication.

Our age also needs a contemporary St. John of the Cross or a Ruysbroeck who will explicate his mystical experiences based on the awareness of his own conscious operations and their dynamic interconnections. In short, we need first-rate mystics who are also intellectually converted to cognitional theory and critical realism.

Summary

In a way reminiscent of Teilhard de Chardin, Lonergan has underscored the intrinsically mystical thrust of the human spirit for ultimate truth, meaning, and value. For Lonergan, this dynamism finds fulfillment through fidelity to the transcendental precepts and surrender to the demands of unrestricted love. Unrestricted mystical love, for Lonergan, is the transcultural constant found in all the world's great religions. His cognitional theory and theological method, grounded in the intellectual, moral, and religious conversion of the authentic subject, provide the foundation required for the contemporary integration of mysticism, theology, and the secular sciences. As noted by Johnston, these could also serve as the basis for a genuine East-West dialogue. His conception of theology consisting of functional specialities correlated to the four levels of consciousness and intentionality, moreover, allows for elaborate interdisciplinary collaboration. Both the new science of mysticism which can integrate contemporary theology, the secular sciences, and Eastern and Western mysticisms, and the future mystical theology redintegrating living spirituality and academic theology have found an auspicious beginning in the writings of Bernard Lonergan.

Epilogue

In a recent book, Richard Woods, O.P. predicts that the mysticism of the future will be characterized by a deeper relationship with the ordinary, integrity, sociality, science and technology, humanism, ecology, ecumenism, and transformation.[1] Because of the undue contemporary emphasis upon unusual states of consciousness, many welcome Woods' focus upon mysticism as being something quite ordinary. While being aware of extraordinary mystical phenomena, Merton, Johnston, Albrecht, Rahner, Lonergan, and others have all focused upon a mysticism of the commonplace, of everyday life, of the mystery of God's love permeating all aspects of human life. This may say much about the future of mysticism.

And as we have already seen, many of these same authors refuse to equate the mystic and the ecstatic. St. Francis de Sales' "ecstasy of work and life,"[2] the extraordinary living out of ordinary life, the deeper and more silent dimension of all authentic human living, needs special emphasis in today's mystical studies. The mystics are important for us today, not because of their extraordinary psychological raptures and ecstasies, but because of the depth at which they live out their daily lives in faith, hope, and love.

Those authors, therefore, who explicate mysticism as a way of life, a way of existing, as a fundamental openness to the mystery of life, a way which may or may not be punctuated by extraordinary experiences, seem to be on the right track. To be sure, some of these authors too easily equate mysticism with religious experience or the spiritual life in general. Still, there is a sense in which mysticism is *radical* religious experience, the very core of the spiritual life, and the heart of authentic human living in both its individual and social aspects.

This radical living may be fostered by the attentive, "noisy contemplation" so well described by William Callahan, S.J.[3] For him, noisy contemplation is "to be like Jesus . . . to be a person who moves in the midst of modern noise and tensions both inside and around us, and who remains aware of others in loving, bonding and caring ways,"[4] a person fully present and committed with attentive love to all aspects of contemporary life.

The "solitary love," the "holy, loving idleness" of bridal mysticism, however, also promotes authentic human living. As St. John of the Cross and others in this profound tradition have pointed out, the attentiveness of love toward God and God alone, for those so called, "is more precious to God and the soul and more beneficial to the Church, even though it seems one is doing nothing, than all these other works put together."[5] This tradition may have been tempted to unholy laziness. The contemporary temptation, however, is to hyper-activism, unenlightened involvement in "causes," and visible results. But, the "folly" of those who know that God is in love with us and who dwell in solitude in this love must not be dismissed as "world-denying," selfish, non-apostolic, and "privatized." Genuine Christianity has always affirmed the value of the bridal mystics who sit at the Lord's feet and do the one thing necessary: love.

As Woods has indicated, integrity, sociality, humanism, and ecology are inextricably linked to the authentic mysticism of the future. The incarnation demonstrates God as a radical humanist whose mystery the mystic experiences and lives. More intense forms of community life should arise from incarnational mysticism. And because the mystic experiences and lives the mystery of the risen life, a more resurrection-centered mysticism would have profound implications for a Christian appreciation of God's one creation, the body, and ecology, for the risen Body is the symbol of the new creation. It would also go far in retrieving the mystical dimensions of the sacraments so deeply tasted in early Christianity.

Because God is in love with us and so loved the world, we are all secretly in love with each other. The genuine mystic also falls in love with God, with the world, and with her fellow human beings. She attempts, therefore, to heal both in her person and through active service today's personal, social, physical, mental, and spiritual fragmentation through integration around the God whose love makes all one. Contemplation-in-action, a mysticism of liberation, a noisy contemplation which "prays" the day, the news, society, and conflicts to promote peace, faith, and justice accomplish this. To be sure, "contemplative prayer is not to be placed at the service of liberation. The aim is rather to open up all its potentialities. . . ."[6] The heart of justice is love which must break open the socio-political, militantly committed, prophetic dimensions of contemplation.

Tomorrow's mysticism, however, must also include "victim soul" or "suffering servant" mysticism. Christ's passion and shameful death, His disgrace, His being misunderstood and rejected, His loneliness and isolation on the Cross, and His entombment were part of our healing, redemption, and transformation. "Victim souls" are not primarily those who suffer the Cross as the setbacks encountered in developing their talents, in promoting social justice, and humanizing the world. They are primarily those who manifest God's hands even in life's apparent absurdities: natural failings, physical defects, accidents, sickness, old age, death, etc. The active mystic of evolution and progress, Teilhard de Chardin, once wrote to his long-time ill sister:

> O Marguerite, my sister, while I, given soul and body to the positive forces of the universe, was wandering over continents and oceans, my whole being passionately taken up in watching the intensification of all the earth's tints and shadows, you were lying motionless, stretched out on your bed of sickness, silently, deep within yourself, transforming into light the world's most grievous shadows. In the eyes of the Creator, which of us, tell me, which of us will have had the better part?[7]

It seems evident that Woods is correct in saying that science and technology are not about to disappear. Teilhard's and Johnston's blending of mysticism, evolution, and the secular sciences, therefore, has more appeal than Merton's and Griffiths' somewhat ambiguous views on science and technology. Albrecht's opening up of the scientific view of mysticism to its non-scientific dimension of mystery, Johnston's call for a new science of mysticism, and Lonergan's method to set the proper base for the collaboration between science and theology are certainly to be praised.

As the intensification of authentic religion, mysticism provides an excellent basis for today's ecumenism. Because deep speaks to deep, the mystics of any tradition recognize a kindred spirit in other traditions. Vatican II has made the dialogue easier by acknowledging the values to be found in the world's great non-Christian religions. Rahner's "anonymous Christian" outlook as well as the "transcultural dimension" underscored by Merton, Johnston, and Lonergan set the stage for a genuine East-West dialogue rooted in mysticism.

We are living in a new age. And if one accepts Karl Rahner's insight that Vatican II's most important achievement was to transform the Church from a European into a world Church, then one has to be aware of contemporary theology's new horizon. It seems impossible to do Christian theology today without paying attention to what the East has to offer. Because of this new horizon, moreover, new questions have arisen which can be answered only by a new mystical theology which learns from the secular sciences and the great non-Christian religions. Both Rahner and Lonergan seem to supply the requisite cutting-edge for the new and future mystical theology.

Many continue to emphasize with Evelyn Underhill that the real sanction of the mystical life, however, is not to be found in experiences, altered states of consciousness, or even the transformation of the person and society. To be sure, these things do flow from mysticism. But the first and last word of mysticism is that only One is holy, the God of Mystery who has given Himself in unconditional love in Jesus' life, death, and resurrection that we may live, die, and rise for each other. The service mystics who find God in all things dramatize the mystery of God's love for the world. Love, therefore, must pour itself out to heal and transform. The bridal mystics dramatize that God is in love with us and that we are all in love with each other. The Christian mystic is an icon of the self-emptying God of love, the crucified and risen Christ. She adumbrates the new creation in which God will be all in all through Christ and in the Spirit of Love.

Notes

Introduction

1. William Ralph Inge, *Christian Mysticism* (New York: Scribner's, 1899).

2. Louis Bouyer, Cong. Orat., "Mysticism/An Essay on the History of the Word," *Understanding Mysticism*, ed. Richard Woods, O.P. (Garden City, N.Y.: Doubleday, 1980) 53.

Chapter 1: Psychological Approaches I

1. William James, *The Varieties of Religious Experience* (New York: New American Library, 1958). Page numbers in the main text refer to this volume.

2. F. C. Happold [*Mysticism. A Study and an Anthology* (Baltimore: Penguin Books, 1971) 46-50] adds the following characteristics of the mystical consciousness: a consciousness of the Oneness of everything, a sense of timelessness, and the feeling that the daily self is somehow unreal.

3. See: Peter Moore, "Mystical Experience, Mystical Doctrine, Mystical Technique," in *Mysticism and Philosophical Analysis*, ed. Steven T. Katz (New York: Oxford University Press, 1978) 101-31; Steven Katz, "Language, Epistemology, and Mysticism," in the same volume, 22-74; Renford Bambrough, "Intuition and the Inexpressible," in the same volume, 200-13.

4. Peter Moore, *art. cit.*, 102-7.

5. *Ibid.*, 105.

6. E. W. Trueman Dicken, *The Crucible of Love* (London, 1963).

7. St. John of the Cross, *The Living Flame of Love* I, 9, 582, in *The Collected Works of St. John of the Cross,* tr. Kieran Kavanaugh, O.C.D. and Otilio Rodriguez, O.C.D. (Washington, D.C.: Institute of Carmelite Studies, 1964).

8. On this point, see: William Hocking, "The Meaning of Mysticism as Seen Through Its Psychology," *op. cit.,* ed. Richard Woods, O.P., 226.

9. See n. 2 above.

10. Steven Katz, *art. cit.,* 22.

11. Carl Keller, "Mystical Literature," *op. cit.,* ed. Stephen Katz, 96.

12. See: Joseph Maréchal, *Studies in the Psychology of the Mystics* (Albany, N.Y.: Magi Books, 1964); Louis Dupré, *The Other Dimension* (Garden City, N.Y.: Doubleday, 1972); Jacques Maritain, *The Degrees of Knowledge* (New York: Charles Scribner's Sons, 1959).

13. See: Harvey D. Egan, S.J., "The Cloud of Unknowing and Pseudo-Mysticism," *Thought* (June, 1979) 162-75.

14. Richard Bucke, *Cosmic Consciousness* (New York: E. P. Dutton, 1969). Page numbers in the main text refer to this volume.

15. Karl Rahner, S.J., *Theology of Death* (New York: Herder and Herder, 1967) 19.

16. Karl Rahner, S.J., *Schriften zur Theologie* 12 (Zurich: Benziger, 1975) 400.

17. Evelyn Underhill, *Mysticism* (New York: E. P. Dutton, 1961) 192-3.

18. Daniel Shine, S.J., ed., *An Interior Metaphysics: The Philosophical Synthesis of Pierre Scheuer, S.J.* (Weston, Mass.: Weston College Press, 1966) 127.

19. Jacques Maritain, "The Natural Mystical Experience and the Void," *op. cit.,* Richard Woods, O.P., ed., 496.

20. *Ibid.,* 497.

21. Walter T. Stace, *The Teachings of the Mystics* (New York: New American Library, 1960). Page numbers in the main text refer to this work. Also see his *Mysticism and Philosophy* (New York: Macmillan, 1960).

22. Steven Katz, *art. cit.*, 26.

23. *Ibid.*, 27.

24. See: Annemarie Schimmel, *Mystical Dimensions of Islam* (Chapel Hill: University of North Carolina, 1975); Robert S. Ellwood Jr., *Mysticism and Religion* (Englewood Cliffs, N.J.: Prentice-Hall, 1980); Geoffrey Parrinder, *Mysticism in the World's Religions* (New York: Oxford University Press, 1976).

25. Steven Katz, *art. cit.*, 46.

26. *Ibid.*, 40. For an excellent treatment of the role of motivation in mysticism, see: William Hocking, *The Meaning of God in Human Experience* (New Haven: Yale University Press, 1963) 341f. and 422f.

27. Peter Moore, "Recent Studies of Mysticism: A Critical Survey," *Religion* (Autumn, 1973) 149.

28. See: Peter Moore, " Mystical Experience, Mystical Doctrine, Mystical Technique," *op. cit.*, ed. Stephen Katz, 119; R. Crookall, *The Interpretation of Cosmic and Mystical Experience* (London, 1961); J. H. M. Whiteman, *The Mystical Life* (London, 1961); Karl Rahner, S.J., "The Ignatian Mysticism of Joy in the World," *Theological Investigations 3* (Baltimore: Helicon, 1967) 279.

29. Peter Moore, *ibid.*, 119.

30. See n. 24 and Georges Morel, *Le Sens de L'Existence selon S. Jean de la Croix,* 3 vols., (Paris: Aubier, 1960-1).

Chapter 2: Psychological Approaches II

1. Erich Neumann, "Mystical Man," *Eranos Jahrbuch* 30 (1968) 375-415. Page numbers in the main text refer to this work.

2. For what many commentators consider an unwarranted identification of psychedelic drug experience with religious mystical experience, see: Aldous Huxley, *The Doors of Perception* (New York: Harper & Row, 1954); Timothy Leary, *The Politics of Ecstasy* (New York: G. P. Putnam, 1968); Alan Watts, *The Joyous Cosmology* (New York: Vintage, 1962). For a more nuanced position, see: Lester Grinspoon and James Bakalar, *Psychedelic Drugs Reconsidered* (New York: Basic Books, 1979); R. E. L. Masters & Jean Houston, *The Varieties of Psychedelic Experience* (New York: Dell, 1966); Stanislav Grof, *Realms of the Unconscious* (New York: E. P. Dutton,

1976). For a fiery refutation of the religious claims made for psyche-delic experience, see: R. C. Zaehner, *Mysticism Sacred and Profane* (New York: Oxford, 1961); *Zen, Drugs, and Mysticism* (New York: Vintage, 1974). The balanced remarks by William Johnston, S.J. [*The Still Point* (New York: Harper & Row, 1970) 143-50] are worth noting.

3. Carl Jung, in his Foreword to D. T. Suzuki's, *An Introduction to Zen Buddhism* (London: Rider, 1969) 15, contends: "The imagination itself is a psychic occurrence, and therefore whether an 'enlightenment' is called 'real' or 'imaginary' is quite immaterial." Erich Fromm's, *Psychoanalysis and Zen Buddhism* (New York: Harper & Row, 1970) 116, gives the counterposition to Jung's "general relativistic position" by emphasizing the need "to differentiate between genuine *satori* experience, in which the acquisition of a new viewpoint is real, and hence true, and a pseudo-experience which can be of a hysterical or psychotic nature. . . ."

4. Peter Moore, "Mystical Experience, Mystical Doctrine, Mystical Technique," *op. cit.*, ed. Stephen Katz, 114. Elmer O'Brien, S.J. [*Varieties of Mystic Experience* (New York: Mentor-Omega, 1965) 16] shows, however, that even with some highly orthodox Christian mystics "the reputed experience does not follow as a doctrinal conclusion from the person's basic philosophic or theological position, but is counter to it."

5. For a position similar to Neumann's on this point, see: Claudio Naranjo & Robert Ornstein, *On the Psychology of Meditation* (New York: Viking Press, 1971) 21.

6. Martin Buber, *Eclipse of God* (New York: Harper & Row, 1957) 80.

7. *Ibid.*, 134. For an excellent, critical appraisal of Jung, see: Victor White, *God and the Unconscious* (Cleveland: World Publishing Co., 1961); *Soul and Psyche* (New York: Harper & Row, 1960).

8. See: Ira Progoff, *The Practice of Process Meditation* (New York: Dialogue House Library, 1980) 11. Friedrich von Hügel [*The Mystical Element of Religion*, 2 vols. (Westminster, Md.: Christian Classics, 1961) I, 65f.] explains how the mystical element in any religion *tends* to suppress the rational, institutional, and historical elements of the religion.

9. John White, ed., *The Highest State of Consciousness* (Garden City, N.Y.: Doubleday, 1972) vii-xvii.

10. *Ibid.*, xii.

11. *Ibid.*, xv.

12. Raymond Prince & Charles Savage, "Mystical States and the Concept of Regression," *op. cit.*, John White, ed., 115.

13. Alexander Maven, "The Mystic Union: A Suggested Biological Interpretation," *op. cit.*, John White, ed., 430.

14. Claire Meyers Owens, "The Mystical Experience: Facts and Values," *op. cit.*, John White, ed., 150.

15. *Ibid.*

16. Kenneth Wapnick, "Mysticism and Schizophrenia," *op. cit.*, John White, ed., 153-74.

17. R. D. Laing, "Transcendental Experience," *op cit.*, John White, ed., 106.

18. Roland Fischer, "On Creative, Psychotic, and Ecstatic States," *op. cit.*, John White, ed., 175.

19. *Ibid.*

20. Arthur Deikman, "Deautomatization and the Mystic Experience," *Altered States of Consciousness*, Charles Tart, ed. (Garden City, N.Y.: Doubleday, 1969) 32.

21. *Ibid.*, 46.

22. See: Abraham Maslow, *Towards a Psychology of Being* (Princeton, N.J.: Van Nostrand, 1962).

23. See: Carl Albrecht, *Psychologie des mystichen Bewusstseins* (Bremen, Germany: Carl Schuenemann Verlag, 1951) and *Das Mystische Erkennen* (Bremen, Germany: Carl Schuenemann Verlag, 1958).

Chapter 3: Irreducibly Plural Types of Mysticisms

1. *Op. cit.*

2. R. C. Zaehner, *Mysticism Sacred and Profane* (New York: Oxford University, 1961). Page numbers in the main text refer to this volume.

3. For a position similar to Huxley's perennial philosophy, see Friedrich Heiler's important "The History of Religions as a Prepara-

tion for the Cooperation of Religions," in *The History of Religions, Essays in Methodology,* ed. by M. Eliade and J. Kitagawa (Chicago: University of Chicago Press, 1959) 142-53.

4. See also: R. C. Zaehner, *Zen, Drugs, and Mysticism* (New York: Random House, 1973).

5. R. C. Zaehner, *Concordant Discord. The Interdependence of Faiths* (Oxford: Clarendon, 1970). Abbreviated as *Discord.*

6. Steven Katz, *op. cit.,* 59.

7. *Discord,* 308.

8. See: Martin Buber, *I and Thou* (New York: Charles Scribner's Sons, 1958). For an overview of Jewish mysticism, see: Gershom Scholem, *op. cit.*

9. Martin Buber, *Between Man and Man* (New York: Macmillan, 1972) 24. Yves Raguin, S.J. [*The Depth of God* (St. Meinrad: Abbey, 1975) 66] also holds this position and says: "The important thing here is to realize that my depth is deeper than I am. But at the same time I may plunge into myself and never find anything more than myself. The self, in fact, is so deep that it can engulf me without my ever realizing there is something further . . . It is easy to see why so many mystics lose themselves in themselves and never meet God."

10. *Discord,* 150-71.

11. Ninian Smart, "Understanding Religious Experience," *op. cit.,* Steven Katz, ed., 13.

12. *Ibid.,* 14.

13. *Ibid.*

14. Ninian Smart, "Interpretation and Mystical Experience, *op. cit.,* Richard Woods, O.P., ed., 84. For an introduction to the main lines of the experience/interpretation controversy, see: Peter Moore, "Recent Studies of Mysticism: A Critical Survey," *op. cit.,* esp. 150-2.

Chapter 4: Mysticism as a Way of Life I

1. Evelyn Underhill, *Mysticism* (New York: E. P. Dutton, 1961). Page numbers in the main text refer to this volume.

2. Quoted by Bernard Lonergan, S.J., *Method in Theology* (New York: Seabury, 1979) 161.

3. See also: Rufus Jones, *Studies in Mystical Religion* (London: Macmillan, 1909) for an excellent presentation of mysticism as a way

of life. The position is well put by William Hocking in "The Meaning of Mysticism as Seen Through Its Psychology," *op. cit.*, Richard Woods, O.P., ed., 224 when he emphasizes "mysticism (primarily) neither as a metaphysics, nor as an experience, but as an art: namely as the fine art . . . of worship."

4. Morton T. Kelsey [*The Other Side of Silence* (Ramsey, N.J.: Paulist, 1976) 134-6, 115] comes very close to calling the apophatic tradition un-Christian. For a fine presentation of the apophatic tradition in the Eastern Christian Church, see: Vladimir Lossky, *The Mystical Theology of the Eastern Church* (Westminster, Md.: Christian Classics, 1973) and George A. Maloney, S.J., *The Mystic of Fire and Light* (Denville, N.J.: Dimension Books, 1975). Also see: Harvey D. Egan, S.J., "Christian Apophatic and Kataphatic Mysticisms," *Theological Studies* (September, 1978) 399-426.

5. For the distinction between a "mysticism of infinity" and a "mysticism of personality," see: Annemarie Schimmel, *op. cit.*, 5. For a strong attack upon the Christian kataphatic tradition, see: Aldous Huxley, *Grey Eminence* (New York: Harper & Row, 1941). See also n. 4.

6. Underhill writes [*op. cit.*, vii] that "no responsible student now identifies the mystic and the ecstatic." Gershom Scholem [*Major Trends in Jewish Mysticism* (New York: Schocken, 1954) 5] also contends that mysticism is more than ecstasy. Agehananda Bharti [*The Light at the Center* (Santa Barbara: Ross-Erikson, 1976)] reduces mysticism to an ecstatic "zero-experience" devoid of all noetic, moral, and religious content. Andrew Greeley [*Ecstasy. A Way of Knowing* (Englewood Cliffs, N.J.: Prentice-Hall, 1974)] likewise equates the mystical and the ecstatic.

7. Annemarie Schimmel [*op. cit.*, 6] also distinguishes between union with God and annihilation in God. Many commentators, however, incorrectly consider the former an inferior type of mysticism.

Chapter 5: Mysticism as a Way of Life II

1. Raymond Bailey, *Thomas Merton on Mysticism* (Garden City, N.Y.: Doubleday, 1975) 12.

2. "The Inner Experience," quoted by Raymond Bailey, *op. cit.*, 151.

3. Thomas Merton, *Contemplative Prayer* (Garden City, N.Y.: Doubleday, 1969) 89.

4. *Ibid.*, 69.

5. *Ibid.*, 108.

6. Thomas Merton, *Zen and the Birds of Appetite* (New York: New Directions, 1968) 55. Abbreviated as *Zen.*

7. *Ibid.*, 12.

8. *Contemplative Prayer,* 114.

9. "The Life That Unifies," *Sisters Today* (1970), Naomi Stone, ed., 65.

10. *Zen,* 71-2.

11. *Thomas Merton Reader* (revised edition), Thomas McDonnell, ed. (Garden City, N.Y.: Doubleday, 1974) 315.

12. "The Inner Experience," quoted by Raymond Bailey, *op. cit.*, 161.

13. *Ibid.*, 168.

14. *Contemplative Prayer,* 90.

15. *Zen,* 125.

16. *Contemplative Prayer,* 90.

17. Thomas Merton, "First Christmas at Gethsemani," *Catholic World* (December, 1979) 30.

18. *Contemplative Prayer,* 97.

19. *Ibid.*, 29.

20. *Ibid.*, 85.

21. *Ibid.*

22. The Benedictine monk, Bede Griffiths, has lived in India for over twenty years. His book, *Return to the Center* (Springfield, Ill.: Templegate, 1977), presents a similarly romantic view of the mystical value of "primitive" living.

23. *Contemplative Prayer,* 39.

24. *Ibid.*, 25.

25. Thomas Merton, *Faith and Violence* (South Bend: University of Notre Dame Press, 1968) 147.

26. Thomas Merton, quoted by E. G. Hinson, "The Catholicization of Contemplation: Thomas Merton's Place in Church Prayer Life," *Perspectives in Religion* (Summer, 1973) 18.

27. "The Inner Experience," quoted by Raymond Bailey, *op. cit.*, 137.

28. *Ibid.*

29. *The Asian Journal of Thomas Merton,* ed. by N. Burton, Bro. P. Hart, J. Laughlin (New York: New Directions, 1969) 312-3.

Chapter 6: Christianity's Eastern Turn

1. *Zen,* 15-32.

2. *The Asian Journal,* 309-10.

3. *Zen,* 44.

4. *The Asian Journal,* 322.

5. Quoted by David Steindal-Rast, "Recollections of Thomas Merton's Last Days in the West," *Monastic Studies* (1969) 10.

6. *Zen,* 36.

7. Thomas Merton, *The Ascent to Truth* (New York: Harcourt Brace and Co., 1951) 285.

8. *Zen,* 24-5.

9. *Ibid.,* 47.

10. *Ibid.,* 4.

11. Thomas Merton, "Two Comments for Forum," *Art and Literature, Collected Essays IV* (Abbey of Gethsemani) 8.

12. *The Asian Journal,* 312.

13. Thomas Merton, *Conjectures of a Guilty Bystander* (Garden City, N.Y.: Doubleday, 1966) 21.

14. See William Johnston, S.J., *The Mysticism of the Cloud of Unknowing* (New York: Desclee Co., 1967) and his editing of: *The Cloud of Unknowing and the Book of Privy Counseling* (Garden City, N.Y.: Doubleday, 1973).

15. Johnston's fellow-Jesuit, Hugo M. Enomiya-Lassalle is another person living a Christianity extended beyond itself. He has been under the direction of a Zen master for some time to experience first-hand Zen's compatibility and/or incompatibility with Christianity. See his: *Zen—Way to Enlightenment* (London: Sheed & Ward, 1966). For someone living this extended Christianity in a Hindu setting in India, see: Bede Griffiths, *op. cit.*

16. For the best single-volume work on this point, see Anthony de Mello, S.J., *Sadhana. A Way to God. Christian Exercises in Eastern Form* (St. Louis: The Institute of Jesuit Sources, 1978).

17. William Johnston, S.J., *The Mirror Mind. Spirituality and Transformation* (=*Mind*) (San Francisco: Harper & Row, 1981) 9.

18. William Johnston, S.J., *The Inner Eye of Love. Mysticism and Religion (=Eye)* (San Francisco: Harper & Row, 1978) 20.

19. *Mind*, 59.

20. William Johnston, S.J., *The Still Point. Reflections on Zen and Christian Mysticism (=Point)* (San Francisco: Harper & Row, 1970) 37.

21. *Ibid.*, 145.

22. *Point*, 138.

23. See: William Johnston, S.J., *Christian Zen* (San Francisco: Harper & Row, 1971) 8.

24. *Point*, 4.

25. *Mind*, 157.

26. See: William Johnston, S.J., *Silent Music. The Science of Meditation (=Music)* (San Francisco: Harper & Row, 1974) 80-91; *Eye*, 90f.

27. *Mind*, 68.

28. *Ibid.*, 39.

29. *Eye*, 132.

30. There seems to be an experiential—not merely an interpretative—difference within Christianity between enlightenment and love mystical experiences. St. Ignatius' famous vision on the banks of the Cardoner River is an example of Christian enlightenment through which he became "another man." St. Teresa of Avila's famous "transverberation" experience of being pierced by God's love is different from her Christian enlightenment experience vision of how all things are in God.

31. *Christian Zen*, 14.

32. For a criticism of Anthony de Mello's *Sadhana* on this point, see: Harvey Egan, S.J., "Prayer and Contemplation as Orthopraxis," *Proceedings of the Catholic Theological Society of America* 35 (1980) 106f.

Chapter 7: Turning East Criticized

1. Quoted by Henri de Lubac, S.J. in, *The Religion of Teilhard de Chardin* (Garden City: Doubleday, 1968) 16.

2. *Ibid.*

3. *Ibid.*

4. Quoted by Ursula King, *Towards a New Mysticism. Teilhard de Chardin and Eastern Religions* (New York: Seabury, 1980) 190.

5. Pierre Teilhard de Chardin, S.J., *The Phenomenon of Man* (New York: Harper & Row, 1959) 33.

6. Quoted by Ursula King in, *op. cit.*, 134.

7. Quoted by C. Cuenot, *Teilhard de Chardin* (Baltimore: Helicon, 1965) 299.

8. Pierre Teilhard de Chardin, S.J., *Writings in Time of War* (New York: Harper & Row, 1968) 29.

9. Pierre Teilhard de Chardin, S.J., *Science and Christ* (New York: Harper & Row, 1968) 104f.

10. *Writings in Time of War*, 29.

11. Quoted by Ursula King in *op. cit.*, 127.

12. Pierre Teilhard de Chardin, S.J., *The Divine Milieu* (New York: Harper & Row, 1960) 116.

13. *Ibid.*, 119.

14. *Ibid.*, 118.

15. Quoted by Ursula King in *op. cit.*, 172.

16. Pierre Teilhard de Chardin, S.J., *Christianity and Evolution* (New York: Harcourt Brace Jovanovich, 1971) 65.

17. Pierre Teilhard de Chardin, S.J., *Letters to Two Friends 1926-1952* (New York: New American Library, 1968) 115.

18. *Writings in Time of War*, 29f.

19. Quoted by Henri de Lubac in *op. cit.*, 171.

20. Pierre Teilhard de Chardin, *Towards the Future* (New York: Harcourt Brace Jovanovich, 1974) 117.

21. Quoted by Ursula King in *op. cit.*, 202-3.

22. *Ibid.*, 158.

23. Pierre Teilhard de Chardin, *Letters to Leontine Zanta* (New York: Harper & Row, 1969) 79.

24. Pierre Teilhard de Chardin, *Letters from a Traveller* (London: Collins, 1962) 86.

25. Pierre Teilhard de Chardin, *How I Believe* (New York: Harper & Row, 1969) 3.

26. Quoted by Ursula King in *op. cit.*, 181.

27. *Writings in Time of War*, 148.

28. *The Divine Milieu*, 123.

29. *Ibid.*, 56.

30. *Ibid.*, 92.

31. *Ibid.*, 104.

32. *Ibid.*, 133.

33. *Ibid.*

34. *Ibid.*, 144.

35. *Ibid.*, 143.

36. *Op. cit.*, 222.

37. Quoted by Ursula King in *op. cit.*, 135.

38. The following comments are a summary of von Balthasar's remarks found in: *In der Fülle des Glaubens. Hans Urs Von Balthasar-Lesebuch*, hrsg. von Medard Kehl und Werner Löser (Freiburg im Breisgau: Herder, 1980) 318-30 and 357-9; Hans Urs von Balthasar, "Catholicism and the Religions," *Communio* 5 (1978) 6-14.

39. Quoted by Thomas Merton, *Zen and the Birds of Appetite*, 62.

40. Harvey Cox, *Turning East* (New York: Simon and Schuster, 1977). Page numbers in the main text refer to this volume.

41. For a cutting, yet often hilarious, account of the exploitation of this Western fascination with the "mystical" India, see: Gita Metha, *Karma Kola. Marketing the Mystic East* (New York: Simon and Schuster, 1979).

Chapter 8: A Contemporary Mystical Theology

1. Karl Rahner, S.J., "Teresa of Avila: Doctor of the Church," *Opportunities for Faith* (New York: Seabury, 1970) 123.

2. Karl Rahner, S.J., *The Dynamic Element in the Church* (New York: Herder and Herder, 1964) 86-7.

3. "Teresa of Avila," *op. cit.*, 125.

4. Karl Rahner, S.J., "Contemplation," *Theological Dictionary* (New York: Herder and Herder, 1965) 99.

5. Karl Rahner, S.J., "The Ignatian Mysticism of Joy in the World," *Theological Investigations 3* (Baltimore: Helicon, 1967) 279. Henceforth, volumes of the *Investigations* will be abbreviated *TI*, followed by the volume number.

6. *Ibid.*, 279-80.

7. Karl Rahner, S.J., "Mysticism," *Encyclopedia of Theology* (=*EOT*) (New York: Seabury, 1975) 1010-11.

8. *Ibid.*, 1011.

9. *The Dynamic Element in the Church*, 147.

10. *Ibid.*, 145.

11. *Ibid.*

12. Karl Rahner, S.J., "Religious Enthusiasm and the Experience of Grace," *TI* 16, 43 and 47.

13. "Teresa of Avila," *op. cit.*, 124-5.

14. *The Dynamic Element in the Church*, 134 n. 28.

15. "Mysticism," *EOT*, 1010.

16. See: Karl Rahner, S.J., "Experience of Self and Experience of God," *TI* 13, 122-32.

17. Karl Rahner, S.J., *On the Theology of Death* (New York: Herder and Herder, 1961) 19.

18. See: Karl Rahner, S.J., "Reflection on the Unity of Love of Neighbour and the Love of God," *TI* 6, 231-49.

19. Karl Rahner, S.J., *Visions and Prophecies* (New York: Herder and Herder, 1964) 14 n. 12.

20. Karl Rahner, S.J., "Everyday Things," *Belief Today* (New York: Sheed and Ward, 1967) 13-43.

21. "Religious Enthusiasm and the Experience of Grace," *op. cit.*, 47.

22. *Vision and Prophecies*, 14 n. 12.

23. *Ibid.*

Chapter 9: A Future Mystical Theology

1. Bernard Lonergan, S.J., *Method in Theology* (New York: Seabury, 1979). Page numbers in the main text refer to this volume.

2. Lonergan highly praises the work done by Robert Doran, S.J. on "psychic conversion," which Lonergan considers a necessary supplement to his own work on intellectual, moral, and religious conversion. See: Robert Doran, S.J., *Subject and Psyche: Ricoeur, Jung, and the Search for Foundations* (Washington, D.C.: University Press of America, 1977); "Subject, Psyche, and Theology's Foundations," *The Journal of Religion* 57/3 (July, 1977) 267-87; "Dramatic

Artistry in the Third Stage of Meaning," *Lonergan Workshop II*, Fred Lawrence (Chico, Cal.: Scholars Press, 1981) 147-99.

3. Bernard Lonergan, S.J., "An Interview with Fr. Bernard Lonergan, S.J.," *A Second Collection*, edited by William F. J. Ryan, S.J. and Bernard J. Tyrell, S.J. (Philadelphia: Westminster, 1974) 230.

4. Lonergan considers the writings of Eric Voegelin very important for grasping the link between mysticism and right order in human existence, especially social life. For an excellent introduction to this profound thinker, see: John Carmody, "Voegelin's Noetic Differentiation: Religious Implications," *Horizons.* 8/2 (Fall, 1981) 223-246.

Epilogue

1. Richard Woods, O.P., *Mysterion. An Approach to Mystical Spirituality* (Chicago: Thomas More Press, 1981) 357-71.

2. St. Francis de Sales, *Treatise on the Love of God* (Rockford: Tan, 1975) vol. 2, 30.

3. William R. Callahan, S.J., "Noisy Contemplation," *The Wind Is Rising. Prayer for Active People*, ed. by William R. Callahan, S.J. and Francine Cardman (Mt. Rainer, Md.: Quixote Center, 1978) 34-7.

4. *Ibid.*, 35.

5. St. John of the Cross, *The Spiritual Canticle, op. cit.*, Stanza 29, #2, 523.

6. Segundo Galilea, "Liberation as the Encounter with Politics and Contemplation," *op. cit.*, Richard Woods, O.P., ed., 534.

7. Quoted by Henri de Lubac, S.J. in *op. cit.*, 263-4.